Spoken Egyptian Arabic

by
Samia Mehrez
Department of Near Eastern Studies
Cornell University

 An Audio-Cassette Course

Especially created to accompany this
book are 12 instructional audio cassettes.
They are available from the publisher.

aUDIO·FORUM

A Division of Jeffrey Norton Publishers, Inc.
Guilford, Connecticut

Spoken Egyptian Arabic

ISBN: 0-88432-536-9   text only
ISBN: 0-88432-131-2   text and cassettes

Published by Audio-Forum,
a division of Jeffrey Norton Publishers, Inc.,
On-The-Green, Guilford, CT 06437

 # Preface

This self-instructional method in Spoken Egyptian
Arabic is the outcome of several years of experience in
teaching Egyptian Arabic in Egypt and the USA. I have
worked with foreign students (American, French, and
Italian) of different backgrounds and interests in
classroom situations, both in Cairo and in the USA. I
have also been the private tutor of both French and
American businessmen in Cairo. These varied experiences
in language teaching convinced me of the need for a
self-sufficient, systematic, beginner's course in
Egyptian Arabic.

The course is primarily concerned with developing
oral rather than written skills. Our assumption is that
the learner's most pressing need is to communicate
orally in everyday situations. The entire text of
Spoken Egyptian Arabic is in transliteration; we do not
introduce Arabic script. The learner's attention should
focus exclusively on mastering a new and intricate
phonetic system. Once that stage of language learning
has been accomplished, the transition to the actual
Arabic script becomes much faster and easier.

Teaching a language to graduate students in a
university is definitely very different from teaching
someone who is already in the business world. This
course is designed to bridge the gap that exists between

highly technical Arabic grammars, meant for the
specialized student of Arabic, and simple phrase-books
of basic sentences that are unsatisfactory for the
purposes of real communication.

Those of you who have some knowledge of Classical
Arabic will find that the presentation of the grammar in
<u>Spoken Egyptian Arabic</u> follows a system akin to that in
other Arabic grammars. Those of you who have no
knowledge of Arabic will find that <u>Spoken Egyptian
Arabic</u> provides a systematic grammar and an easy
introduction to Classical Arabic should you decide to
continue with the language.

This course has been tested with a group of foreign
engineers and businessmen in Cairo and the tapes have
been used in the language laboratory with groups of
foreign university students. All groups found that
working with the tapes and the transcriptions
accelerated the learning process to a great extent.

I would like to take this opportunity to express my
deepest gratitude to Mr. Donald D. Johnson of Rockwell
International, an American businessman in Cairo, who
inspired the idea of this self-instructional course in
Spoken Egyptian. Mr. Johnson's encouragement during the
developmental stages, his continued enthusiasm and
support, have helped make this course a reality.

Thanks are also due to Professor Claude-France
Audebert, the director of the Center for Intensive Study
of Arabic in Cairo and Professor of Arabic at the
University of Aix-en-Provence in France. Professor

Audebert's consistent guidance and her comments on the manuscript have been a great help in improving the whole structure of the course.

I would also like to extend my thanks to all the people who have been involved in the actual production of this course both in Cairo and at Cornell University in the USA. I am very grateful for their assistance, patience and cooperation.

October 1984

Samia Mehrez
Cornell University
Ithaca, New York

 # Notes to Learner

Egyptian Arabic has become the most widely
understood dialect in the Arabic speaking world.
Egyptian movies, songs, television series and millions
of Egyptian expatriate professionals and labourers have
spread the dialect throughout the rest of the Arab
World. Any person who speaks Egyptian Arabic will have
virtually no problem communicating with Arabs anywhere.

Spoken Egyptian Arabic is an introductory, self-
instructional method in the spoken dialect of Cairo.
The course includes a textbook and twelve cassette
tapes.

As with any other foreign language, learning Arabic
means developing a new set of speech habits, and using a
sound system different from English. To facilitate this
process, our textbook includes transcriptions of all the
material recorded on the tapes. You will be able to
listen, repeat and correct yourself with the aid of the
transcriptions.

Our primary aim is to enable the student to
communicate with Arabic speakers in the shortest
possible time. We therefore use a phonetic system to
spare the student the time and energy spent on
mastering the intricacies of the Arabic script.

As you begin your study of Arabic, remember:
1.   To learn a language effectively you need to follow

these four steps:

    a. listen; b. imitate; c. repeat; d. memorize.

2. Work slowly. It is tempting to rush through the material, but learning a language is a step-by-step process. Taking the time to master the first steps will enable you to learn faster later.

3. The material is presented in a systematic manner. If you overlook something in any lesson it will remain a problem forever. Make sure you have mastered all the items in one lesson before you move on to the next.

4. Record yourself from time to time. Compare your pronunciation, intonation, and stress with that on the tapes. Try doing your drills aloud.

5. When you feel that you can take no more, take a break--but for no more than a day or two. Languages fade fast.

6. As the material builds up, your feeling of progress will slow down. Do not feel defeated. Learning a language is like a marathon--the ones who succeed are the ones who keep going.

MATERIALS FOR THE COURSE

I. <u>THE TEXTBOOK</u>

The textbook is composed of thirteen units. Units One through Twelve include grammatical notes and transcriptions of the drills on the cassette tapes. Unit Thirteen includes a collection of short dialogues and narrative texts that the student can

use for self-testing throughout the course. You
should read the first text in Unit Thirteen after
you have mastered the material in Unit One; the
second text after you have mastered Unit Two, etc.
until you have covered all twelve (and therefore
thirteen) units. The material in Unit Thirteen
increases in difficulty to match the increasing
grammatical complexity of the other twelve units.

II.   THE TAPES

There are twelve cassette tapes in this course.
The tapes are all in Arabic. Instructions for the
drills are in English and are both recorded on the
tapes and written in the text. To maximize your
benefit from Spoken Egyptian Arabic we urge you to
use the written and taped material together. Read
the grammatical sections in each unit before
beginning the drills on the corresponding cassette
tape. Do not forget to go to Unit Thirteen for a
test every time you complete a unit.

Table of Contents

TAPE 12 (Unit 13)

Everyday Expressions
Expressions of Time
Names of Professions
Names of Places
Countries and Nationalities
Fruits, Vegetables and Groceries
Public Services
Means of Transportation

Introductory Chapter

Transliteration System

There are certain sounds in Arabic that may not exist in your native tongue. You may never have used your vocal chords to produce them. We have therefore created symbols to allow you to recognize these new sounds. A transliteration system allows you to write words as you hear natives pronounce them. It also allows you to reproduce words like a native would. It is to your advantage to spend time on this early section. It will facilitate your learning experience in the long run. The following are lists of consonants and vowels. They are recorded on tape. At this point in the course concentrate on mastering the new sounds.

TAPE I/SIDE 1

List of Consonants

Please Listen and Repeat:

Consonant	Example
'	su'aal, ti'iil, mas'uul
b	bokrà, bint, badla
d	da, dool, daras
ḍ	dàrb, idràb
f	fostaan, fatla
g	gidiid, gazma
ġ	ġada, loġa, ġariib
ç	çàràbiyyà, çàràb, saaça
h	hoduum, hàràm, àhrààm

1

Consonant	Examples
h	háráámi, ilhisaab, garh
k	kalaam, itkallim
l	lókándá, fuul, lahma
m	moskila, imbaarih, mábruuk
n	innáhárdá, naas, insaan
r	rikib, rádio
s	Samia, ismi
s	sáráf, seef, noss
$	$okrán, mota$akkir, $oft
t	tilifoon, itneen, taani
t	táláb, táálib, táyyáárá
w	waziir, walad, wadda
y	yareet, yasmiin, kobbaaya
z	ziyáárá, zamaan, zamaalik
z	zárf, záriif
q	qor'áán, ilqááhirá
x	xárág, xáális, xawaaga

TAPE I/SIDE 1

Contrast Between a Short Vowel (V) and a Long Vowel (VV).

Please Listen and Repeat

i	fihim, tiliç, nizil
ii	záriif, táwiil, nidiif
a	fatah, daxal, sa'al
aa	daaxil, faahim, çaarif

2

u	ṣoftu, kaanu, kuntu
uu	ṣuufu, mamnuuç, mas'uul
ee	feen, beet, beedȧ
o	montazah, moftaah, fostaan
oo	loon, bȧntȧloon, mooz
ȧ	fȧsolyȧ, fȧziiç, itfȧddȧl
ȧȧ	fȧȧr, fȧȧtir, fȧȧsil

TAPE I/SIDE 1

Contrast Between the Consonants

t/ṭ   h/ḥ   s/ṣ   z/ẓ   '/ç   ġ/x   d/ḍ

Please Listen and Repeat

t/ṭ	taab / ṭȧȧb
	tiin / ṭiin
h/ḥ	ḥȧrȧm / ḥȧrȧȧm
	howwa / hawwa
s/ṣ	salla / ṣȧllȧ
	simsȧȧr / sorṣȧȧr
z/ẓ	waziir / ẓȧriif
	mazȧhr / mȧẓhȧr
'/ç	alli / çaali
ġ/x	ġadda / xalla
	ġiyȧȧr / xiyȧȧr
d/ḍ	darb / ḍȧrb
	dafaç / ḍȧȧç

TAPE I/SIDE 1

Doubled Consonants

Please Listen and Repeat

màrà	màrrà
wàrà	warra
wàsàl	wàssàl
dafaç	daffaç
daxal	daxxal
kàsàr	kàssàr
alaç	allaç
noss	bass
ràdd	habb
dàll	foll
koll	ʃamm
lamm	za"
nidif	nàddàf
fihim	fahhim
nisi	nassa

TAPE I/SIDE 1

Dictation

Please listen to the following list and write the words
down as you hear them. After you finish the dictation,
check the correct spelling from the list below. The
dictation will help you discover which sounds you are
not hearing correctly. If you have problems with the
dictation you should listen to the tape once more, and
then take the dictation. Now begin:

Word	Meaning
çàràbiyyà	car
ilhisaab	the cheque, the bill
seef	summer
warra	to show
koll	every, all
noss	half
sàáhib	friend (m. s.)
imbaariḥ	yesterday
dilwa'ti	now
xawaaga	foreigner
ġada	lunch
saaça	hour, watch
çaṣa	dinner
hawaali	approximately
ta'riiban	approximately
su'aal	question
çala	on
da'aayi'	minutes

NOTE: There are no words in Arabic that begin with a vowel. All the vowels you see in the English script are " ' ".

The Definite Article "il"

The definite article "il" means "the." To make any common noun definite in Arabic we add to it the definite article "il." Proper nouns, i.e., the names of people, places, and countries, do not take the article since they are already definite. The word "bint" means "girl." To make this word definite, i.e., "the girl" instead of "a girl" we add the definite article in front of the noun. For example:

il bint   ilbint

The Definite Article "il"

Make the Following Words Definite:

walad	a boy	ilwalad	the boy
badla	a suit	ilbadla	the suit
fostaan	a dress	ilfostaan	the dress
bàntàloon	trousers	ilbàntàloon	the trousers
beet	a house	ilbeet	the house, home
ism	a name	il'ism	the name
hoduum	clothes	ilhoduum	the clothes
madrasa	school	ilmadrasa	the school
xawaaga	a foreigner	ilxawaaga	the foreigner
çàràbiyyà	a car	ilçàràbiyyà	the car

Assimilation of the Definite Article:

Arabic consonants are divided into two groups: sun and moon letters. If a word begins with a moon letter, the definite article is simply added to the word. If a word begins with a sun letter, the definite article becomes assimilated. The letter "s" is a sun letter. The word "sitt" means "woman." To make this word definite we would say "issitt" rather than "ilsitt." We drop the "l" of the article and double the sun letter "s" with which the word begins.

The following is a list of the sun and moon letters:

Moon Letters	Sun Letters
'	d
b	ḍ
f	g
ġ	k
ç	l
h	n
ḥ	r
m	s
w	ṣ
y	ş
q	t
x	ṭ
	z
	ẓ

TAPE I/SIDE 1

Assimilation of the Definite Article

Please Listen and Repeat

Arabic	English	Arabic	English
ḍeef	a guest	iḍḍeef	the guest
dars	a lesson	iddars	the lesson
gidiid	new	iggidiid	the new
gazma	shoe	iggazma	the shoe
kalaam	words	ikkalaam	the words

7

Arabic	English	Arabic	English
korsi	chair	ikkorsi	the chair
laḥma	meat	illaḥma	the meat
naas	people	innaas	the people
raagil	a man	irraagil	the man
sana	a year	issana	the year
sitt	a woman	issitt	the woman
ʃaariҫ	a street	iʃʃaariҫ	the street
ʃàhr	a month	iʃʃàhr	the month
tilifoon	a telephone	ittilifoon	the telephone
tàffàáyà	an ashtray	ittàffàáyà	the ashtray
zàrf	an envelope	izzàrf	the envelope

Make the Following Words Definite

(Not on tape)

madrasa	school	ilmadrasa
lokàndà	hotel	illokàndà
hàràm	pyramid	ilhàràm
ʃaariҫ	street	iʃʃaariҫ
gazma	shoe	iggazma
walad	boy	ilwalad
sitt	woman	issitt
raagil	man	irraagil
tilifoon	telephone	ittilifoon
naas	people	innaas
ʃa''a	apartment	iʃʃ''a
xawaaga	foreigner	ilxawaaga
fitàar	breakfast	ilfitàar

The Helping Vowel

In spoken Egyptian Arabic, the sequence of three consonants (CCC) is absolutely not permissible. A helping vowel is inserted to break the sequence CCC. The helping vowel is basically an "E" sound which is added after the second consonant in the sequence CCC. For example:

noss E noss   "half half," i.e., "so so"

TAPE I/SIDE 1

The Helping Vowel

Add the Helping Vowel and Repeat

noss	noss	half half
bint	kibiira	big girl
abl	Mona	before Mona
baçd	sana	after a year
gamb	Mohamed	beside Mohamed
wa't	taani	another time
koll	yoom	every day
noss	saaça	half an hour

NOTE: Remember to insert the "E" sound for yourself whenever you see CCC arising between two words. The "E" will not appear in our material.

The sequence CCC may arise within the same word. This often happens when we join a noun and a suffix pronoun. For example:

ism (name)   hom (them)

9

The word "ism" alone means "name." When we join it with "hom," which is a suffix pronoun, we are saying "their name." "ism" is a word that ends in two CC and "hom" begins with a C. If we join them together we would have the sequence CCC. In order to avoid that, we will use a helping vowel within the same word. Instead of saying "ismhom," we will say "ismohom." We add a helping vowel. In cases like this, where we are using a helping vowel internally, the vowel itself will vary, i.e., a/ i/ o/ u. Here are some examples:

gamb (beside)   ha   (her)   gambaha

abl (before)   na   (us)   ablina

You will see more of the internal helping vowels once we begin the possessive pronouns and also the verb conjugations.

Stress

Stress in Egyptian Arabic varies according to the structure of the word itself. There are three basic rules:

1. Stress falls on the next to last syllable if the word consists of more than two syllables.

2. If the word is a two syllable word, stress falls on the first syllable.

3. Stress will fall on the last syllable if that syllable includes a long vowel, or if the word ends in a double consonant.

Presenting Oneself

The Personal Pronouns

TAPE I/SIDE 2

The Personal Pronouns

Please Listen and Repeat

ana Samia	I am Samia.
inta John	You are John.
inti Nancy	You are Nancy.
howwa Mohamed	He is Mohamed.
hiyya Mona	She is Mona.
ihna Samia we John	We are Samia and John.
intu Nancy we Mohamed	You are Nancy and Mohamed.
homma Samia we John we Nancy	They are Samia, John and Nancy.

Now Repeat Them Once More.

ana	I	(m./f. s.)
inta	you	(m. s.)
inti	you	(f. s.)
howwa	he	(m. s)
hiyya	she	(f. s.)
ihna	we	(m./f. pl.)
intu	you	(m./f. pl.)
homma	they	(m./f. pl.)

Translate the Following

I am Nancy.	ana Nancy
She is Mona.	hiyya Mona
We are Nancy and Mona.	ihna Nancy we Mona
He is John.	howwa John
You are Mohamed.	inta Mohamed
You are John and Mohamed.	intu John we Mohamed
They are Mona and John.	homma Mona we John

Translate the Following

He is John and I am Nancy.

She is Mona and he is Mohamed.

They are Mona and Samia and you are John.

You are John and Mohamed and we are Samia and Mona.

You are John and you are Nancy.

How to Ask Questions

"I am Samia" is a statement. There are three possible ways of formulating questions for such a statement:

1. By intonation:

You are Samia?	inti Samia?
Yes, I am Samia	aywa, ana Samia
No, I am Mona.	la', ana Mona

2. By using a pure interrogative:

Who are you?	inti miin?
I am Samia.	ana Samia
Who are they?	homma miin?
They are John and Nancy.	homma John we Nancy

3. By making a statement and adding "mi$ kida" at the end of the statement:

inta Mohamed, mi$ kida?

You are Mohamed, isn't it so?

inti Samia, mi$ kida?

You are Samia, isn't it so?

New Words:

aywa	yes
la'	no
miin	who
mi$ kida	isn't it so?

TAPE I/SIDE 2

How to Ask Questions

Translate the Questions Then Answer Them

Who are you?   inta miin?   ana Mohamed

Now Begin

Who is she?	(Mona)
Who are they?	(Mona and Nancy)
Who is he?	(Mohamed)
Who are you?	(Samia)

13

Who are you?   (John)

Who are you?   (Samia and Mohamed)

TAPE I/SIDE 2

Formulate Questions Using Intonation

1. La', ana Mona

2. Aywa ihna Samia we Mohamed

3. Aywa howwa John we hiyya Nancy

4. La', ana Nancy we hiyya Mona

Repeat the Drill Using a Statement that Ends with "miş kida?"

Answers:

Using Intonation

1. inti Samia?

2. intu Samia we Mohamed?

3. howwa John we hiyya Nancy?

4. inti Mona we hiyya Nancy?

Using "mişkida"

1. inti Samia, miş kida?

2. intu Samia we Mohamed miş kida?

3. howwa John we hiyya Mona, miş kida?

4. inti Mona we hiyya Nancy, miş kida?

Expression of Existence

Like many other languages, English uses the verb "to be" in the present tense to express the existence of a thing or person in the present. "I am Samia" is an expression of existence. "Kaan" is the verb "to be" in Arabic. However, it is an auxiliary verb and we will see its uses in the coming lessons. Expression of existence in the present in Arabic is conveyed through a nominal sentence. It is called "nominal" because it contains no verb. It translates, however, as if it contained the verb "to be" in the present. For example:

     ana Samia   I am Samia.

The Arabic sentence contains no verb.

More Examples:

Mona bint	Mona is a girl.
Mohamed walad	Mohamed is a boy.
howwa masri	He is Egyptian.
hiyya masriyya	She is Egyptian.
homma fi masr	They are in Egypt.
ihna fi amriica	We are in the U.S.A.

TAPE I/SIDE 2

Expression of Existence

Replace the Subject with a Pronoun Then Translate the Sentence

1.   Mona fi masr   hiyya fi masr

      She is in Egypt.

2.   Mohamed fi lbeet   howwa fi lbeet

      He is at home.

3. Mona we Samia fi lꜥàràbiyyà   homma fi lꜥàràbiyyà
   They are in the car.

4. ana we John fi màsr   ihna fi màsr
   We are in Egypt.

5. Mohamed fi llokàndà   howwa fi llokàndà
   He is at the hotel.

6. inta we Samia fi lbeet   intu fi lbeet
   You are at home.

TAPE I/SIDE 2

Convert the Statements Above into Intonation Questions
Then Answer Them Using a Pronoun.   Here is an example:

   Mona fi màsr?

   aywa, hiyya fi màsr

TAPE I/SIDE 2

Ask Questions with "miš kida" Using the Sentences Above

   Mona fi màsr, miš kida?

   aywa hiyya fi màsr

TAPE I/SIDE 2

Dictation

   Listen to the tape. There are no transcriptions
for this section. Check your answers from Unit I.

TAPE I/SIDE 2

Translation

(Not on tape)

Listen to the dictation on tape. Translate the
sentences into English.

Pointing Things Out

The Demonstrative

TAPE II/SIDE 1

The Demonstrative

Please Listen and Repeat

di bint	This is a girl.
di lbint	This is the girl.
da walad	This is a boy.
da lwalad	This is the boy.
dool awlaad	These are boys.
dool il'awlaad	These are the boys.

A demonstrative means "this." In English we say "this" if the thing or person to which we are pointing is nearby. We say "that" if the thing to which we are pointing is far away. In spoken Egyptian, however, we do not have this distinction. There are three demonstratives:

da   masculine singular
di   feminine singular
dool plural (feminine/masculine)

1. The demonstrative agrees with the noun to which it refers. If the noun is masculine singular, the demonstrative will also be masculine singular:

    da maktab   This is an office.

    If the noun if feminine singular, the demonstrative will also be feminine singular:

    di Samia   This is Samia.

19

If the noun is a human plural (feminine or masculine), the demonstrative will agree with it in number:

dool awlaad   These are boys.

dool banaat   These are girls.

2. All non-human plurals are treated like feminine singular nouns. Therefore, they take the feminine singular demonstrative "di."

lokåndå	hotel
lokåndåat	hotels
di lokåndåat	These are hotels.
çåråbiyyå	car
çåråbiyyåat	cars
di çåråbiyyåat	These are cars.

How to Ask Questions Using Demonstratives:

1. If the statement is "di çåråbiyyå" (this is a car), then how can we ask a question?

eeh di?   What is this?

di çåråbiyyå   This is a car.

"eeh," which means "what," is used to ask questions about things.

2. If the statement is "di Samia" or "da Mohamed," then what is the question?

miin di?   di Samia

miin da?   da Mohamed

"miin," which means "who," is used to ask questions about people.

The Presentational Particle

Like the demonstrative we have three particles:

aho	masculine singular
ahe	feminine singular
ahom	plural (feminine/masculine)

A _presentational particle_ is used to _present_ things or persons as one is pointing to them:

aho lmaktab   Here is the office.

Again, when we present things in English we say "here" when the thing is nearby and "there" when the thing is far away. Spoken Egyptian does not have this distinction.

TAPE II/SIDE 1

The Presentational Particle

Please Listen and Repeat

aho lbeet	Here is the house.
ahe llokåndå	Here is the hotel.
ahom il'awlaad	Here are the boys.

1. The presentational particle _usually_ appears at the beginning of the sentence _before_ the noun it is presenting.

2. Like the demonstrative, the presentational particle agrees with the noun it is presenting. (Refer to the examples above.)

3. All non-human plurals take the presentational particle "ahe" since they are treated as feminine singular nouns.

   çåråbiyyå   car

çàràbiyyààt   cars
ahe lçàràbiyyààt   Here are the cars.

Questions Using the Presentational Particle:

If the statement is

aho lmaktab   Here is the office.

then the question will be

<u>feen</u> il maktab?   <u>Where</u> is the office?

NOTE:

Instead of saying:
di   ilbint   we say: di   lbint
Instead of:
da   ilbeet   we say: da   lbeet

There is a simple explanation for dropping the "i" on the definite article. The word just before it ends in a vowel. Instead of pronouncing the two vowels we assimilate them:

da   ilmaktab   da   lmaktab

Notice that we did not drop the "i" of the definite article with "dool" or "ahom" because they both end in consonants and we do not have the difficult sequence of two vowels. We do not assimilate:

dool ilbanaat   These are the girls.
<u>but</u>
di lbint   This is the girl.
ahom ilbanaat   Here are the girls.
<u>but</u>
ahe lbint   Here is the girl.

Describing People, Places and Things

Types of Nouns

Singular Nouns: Masculine/Feminine

1. Masculine Nouns:

Masculine singular nouns predominantly end in a consonant. Here are some examples:

TAPE II/SIDE 1

Please Listen and Repeat

maktab	office/desk
beet	house/home
råågil *Rogel*	man
ƃaariç	street
modiir	manager
rå'iis	president
waziir	minister
sawwaa'	driver
ba''aal	grocer
mohandis	engineer
mowåzzåf	employee
ƃaay	tea

Some masculine nouns end in a vowel. A small group among them end in the vowel "a." These are not to be confused with the feminine ending "a" with which we will deal presently. Here are some examples:

Nouns that End in a Vowel

Please Listen and Repeat

mabna	building
korsi	chair
tarzi	tailor
abu	father of someone
axu *aho*	brother of someone

2.   ## Feminine Nouns

Feminine singular nouns are marked by the feminine ending "a" which distinguishes them from the masculine nouns. Here are some examples:

Please Listen and Repeat:

ša''a	apartment
širka	company
šàntà	bag/suitcase/purse
gazma	shoe
badla	suit
ööda	room
kobbaaya	glass
wallaaça	lighter
sigàárà	cigarette
tàffààyà	ashtray
izaaza	bottle
ahwa	coffee

REMARKS:

1. Names of professions exist in both forms: masculine and feminine. The masculine form of the noun is transformed into feminine by simply adding the feminine ending "a" to the masculine noun. Here are some examples:

TAPE II/SIDE 1

Masculine and Feminine Nouns

Please Listen and Repeat

modiir	manager	modiira
mohandis	engineer	mohandisa
doktoor	doctor	doktoora
tåålib	student	tååliba
çaamil	worker	çaamila
ostaaz	professor	ostaaza
waziir	minister	waziira
ẓaġġaal	servant	ẓaġġaala
modarris	teacher	modarrisa

2. Some family relations also exist in both forms. The masculine is transformed into feminine by adding the feminine ending "a" to the masculine. Here are some examples:

TAPE II/SIDE 1

Relatives: Masculine and Feminine

Please Listen and Repeat

| xaal | maternal uncle | xaala | maternal aunt |

çamm	paternal uncle	çamma	paternal aunt
gidd	grand father	gidda	grand mother

3. It is not always possible to transform nouns into the feminine by adding the feminine ending "a" to the masculine noun. The words are totally different.

4. All countries are treated as feminine nouns whether or not they end in an "a." If we want to use a demonstrative with countries, we will always use "di"

di màsr	This is Egypt.
di amriika	This is America.
di lyabaan	This is Japan.

5. Very few words are feminine words which do not have the feminine ending "a." Here are some examples:

bint	girl
sitt	woman
oxt	sister
omm	mother
balad	country

6. Not all words that end in an "a" are feminine singular nouns. This "a" is sometimes a vowel and not a feminine ending. This is true of some verbs, prepositions and masculine nouns. Here are some examples:

Prepositions:

maça	with
wàrà	behind
wayya	with

Verbs:

bana	to build

26

kawa	to press clothes
la'a	to find

Masculine Nouns:

osaama	(proper name)
mabna	building

Plurals of Nouns

In Arabic there are two basic kinds of plurals:

1. Sound Plurals

2. Broken Plurals

1. Sound Plurals

They are formed by adding a suffix to the singular word. We have two kinds of sound plurals:

a. Sound Feminine Plural: (-aat)

Many words form their plural by adding the suffix (-aat) to the singular word. There are many feminine singular words that do not take the sound feminine plural suffix (-aat). Their plural exists in other patterns that we will see presently.

TAPE II/SIDE 1

Sound Feminine Plural

Please Listen and Repeat

di	mohandisa	engineer (f.)	dool	mohandisaat
di	mowàzzàfà	employee (f.)	dool	mowàzzàfààt
di	wizààrà	ministry (f.)	di	wizàrààt

27

di	kobbaaya	glass (f.)	di	kobbayaat
di	wallaaᶜa	lighter (f.)	di	wallaᶜaat
di	tåråbéezå	table (f.)	di	tåråbezåat
di	lokåndå	hotel (f.)	di	lokåndåat
da	båntåloon	trousers (m.)	di	båntålonåat
da	tamriín	exercise (m.)	di	tamriínaat

b. <u>Sound Masculine Plural</u>: (-iin)

Many words form their plural by simply adding the
suffix (-iin) to the singular word. There are many
masculine singular words that do not take the sound
masculine plural suffix (-iin). Their plural
exists in other patterns that we will see
presently.

TAPE II/SIDE 1

<u>Sound Masculine Plural</u>

<u>Please Listen and Repeat</u>

da	mohandis	engineer (m.)	dool	mohandisiin
da	mowåzzåf	employee (m.)	dool	mowåzzåfiin
da	ba''aal	grocer	dool	ba''aliin
da	bayyaaᶜ	vender	dool	bayyaᶜiin
da	sawwaa'	driver	dool	sawwa'iin
da	ʂayyaal	porter	dool	ʂayyaliin
da	bawwaab	doorman	dool	bawwabiin

2. <u>Broken Plurals</u>:

Broken plurals are irregular. Many words in
Arabic do not take (-aat) or (-iin) to form their
plurals. Their plurals are formed by using other

patterns. In the case of broken plurals, the
singular word changes somewhat. It is not a simple
process whereby we simply add a suffix like (-aat)
or (-iin) to the singular form. There are numerous
patterns of broken plurals in Arabic. The problem
is that they are many, and it is quite difficult to
predict what plural pattern a singular word will
take.

There are many rules for broken plural
patterns. We will give you groups of words to
demonstrate some of the most common broken plural
patterns. Familiarize yourself with the <u>sound</u> of
the singular word. With practice, you will
discover that many singular words that <u>sound</u> alike
take the same broken plural pattern.

TAPE II/SIDE 1

Broken Plurals

<u>Please Listen and Repeat</u>

<u>Singular</u>		<u>Plural</u>
maktab	office/desk	makaatib
mo∮kila	problem	ma∮aakil
måsråh	theatre	masaarih
∮aariç	street	∮awaariç
mabna	building	mabaani
korsi	chair	karaasi
madrasa	school	madaaris
måsnåç	factory	måsååniç
∮ibbaak	window	∮ababiik
moftaah	key	mafatiih
fostaan	dress	fasatiin
måwduuç	subject	måwådiiç

Singular		Plural
makwagi	dry cleaner	makwagiyya
tarzi	tailor	tarziyya
bostågi	mail man	bostågiyya
sånåyçi	artisan	sånåyçiyya
sofrågi	butler	sofrågiyya
badla	suit	bidal
nimra	number	nimar
nokta	joke	nokat
¢åntå	bag/suitcase	¢onåt
fatla	string	fital
gazma	shoe	gizam
¢a''a	apartment	¢u'a'
forså	chance	forås
oodå	room	owåd
beet	house	beyuut
bank	bank	benuuk
rå''iis	president	ro'åså
waziir	minister	wozårå
doktoor	doctor	dakatra
ostaaz	professor	asatza
kaatib	clerk/writer	kataba
tåålib	student	tålåbå

REMARKS:

1. We will always provide you with the plural forms
   since they are not predictable.

2. Please make a point of _learning_ plurals because
   they are difficult to guess.

3. Whenever someone gives you a new word ask for its plural form and learn it along with the new word.

TAPE II/SIDE 1

Agreement Between Nouns and Demonstratives

Use the Correct Demonstrative In Front of the Following

Nouns, then Translate the Sentence:

1. ȼaariȼ   da ȼaariȼ   (This is a street.)
2. lokåndå   di lokåndå
3. måsr   di måsr
4. ȼåråbiyyå   di ȼåråbiyyå
5. mohandisaat   dool mohandisaat
6. tilifonaat   di tilifonaat
7. båntålonååt   di båntålonååt
8. beet   da beet
9. ȼa''a   di ȼa''a
10. makwagiyya   dool makwagiyya

Repeat the drill, making the words definite by adding "il." Remember the sun and moon letters. Keep in mind that if the word before "il" ends in a vowel, you will drop the "i" on "il." Here is an example:

   di ilbint   di lbint

1. da ȼaariȼ   da ȼȼaariȼ
2. di lokåndå   di llokåndå
3. di måsr   di måsr
4. di ȼåråbiyyå   di lȼåråbiyyå
5. dool mohandisaat   dool ilmohandisaat
6. da beet   da lbeet
7. di tilifonaat   di ttilifonaat

31

Adjectives

1. Adjectives, like nouns, have masculine, feminine and plural forms.

2. Like nouns, they also have broken plural patterns to which we will introduce you.

3. Adjectives agree with the nouns they are qualifying:

   a. in gender (feminine/masculine)
   b. iń definiteness ("il").

4. Adjectives always <u>follow</u> the nouns they are qualifying. Here are some examples:

TAPE II/SIDE 1

Order of Nouns and Adjectives

Please Listen and Repeat

bint tȧwiilȧ	a tall girl
walad tȧwiil	a tall boy
ilbanaat ittowȧȧl	the tall girls

5. Adjectives have <u>one</u> plural form that is used for both feminine and masculine plural nouns. For example:

TAPE II/SIDE 1

Plural Adjectives

Please Listen and Repeat

mohandisiin ẓȧtriin

mohandisaat ẓȧtriin

mowȧzzȧfiin ẓȧtriin

mowȧzzȧfȧȧt ẓȧtriin

32

6. Non-human plurals are treated like feminine singular nouns. They take feminine singular adjectives.

TAPE II/SIDE 1

Non-human Plurals

Please Listen and Repeat

ɕaariҫ waasiҫ	a wide street
ɕawaariҫ wasҫa	wide streets
lokåndå gidiida	a new hotel
lokåndååt gidiida	new hotels
beet kibiir	a big house
beyuut kibiira	big houses

TAPE II/SIDE 2

List of Adjectives

Masculine, Feminine and Plural Forms.

Masculine	Feminine	Plural
kibiir (big)	kibiira	kobaar
tåwiil (tall)	tåwiilå	towåål
gidiid (new)	gidiida	godaad
adiim (old)	adiima	odaam
zåriif (nice)	zåriifå	zorååf
gamiil (beautiful)	gamiila	gomaal
ti'iil (heavy)	ti'iila	to'aal
xafiif (light weight)	xafiifa	xofaaf
rixiis (cheap)	rixiiså	roxåås
nidiif (clean)	nidiifå	nodååf

33

Masculine	Feminine	Plural
waasiç (wide)	wasça	wasçiin
dayya' (narrow)	dayya'a	dayya'iin
mohimm (important)	mohimma	mohimmiin
fȧȧdi (empty)	fȧdyȧ	fȧdyiin
malyaan (full)	malyana	malyaniin
soġȧyyȧr (small)	soġȧyyȧrȧ	soġȧyyȧriin
osȧyyȧr (short)	osȧyyȧrȧ	osȧyyȧriin
ġaali (expensive)	ġalya	ġalyiin
kaslaan (lazy)	kaslaana	kaslaniin
taçban (tire)	taçbaana	taçbaniin
zaçlaan (upset)	zaçlaana	zaçbaniin
gaçaan (hungry)	gaçaana	gaçaniin
çȧtȿȧȧn (thirsty)	çȧtȿȧȧnȧ	çȧtȿȧniin
ȿabçaan (full stomach)	ȿabçaana	ȿabçaniin
dawȿa (noisy)	dawȿa	dawȿa
zahma (crowded)	zahma	zahma
sahl (easy)	sahla	sahl
sȧçb (difficult)	sȧçbȧ	sȧçb

Review

1. Demonstratives:

    da
    di
    dool

    How to Ask Questions:

What is this?	eeh da?
Who is this?	miin da?

2. Presentational Particles:

    aho
    ahe
    ahom

34

How to Ask Questions:

feen ----- ?
where is -----?

3. Non-human plurals are treated like feminine
   singular nouns. Therefore, they take feminine
   singular demonstrative and feminine singular
   presentational particles.

4. Nouns:

   a. Singular

   masculine   feminine

   predominantly   predominantly
   end in consonant   end in feminine "a"

   b. Plural

   sound   broken

   regular (-aat)+(-iin)   several patterns

5. Adjectives:

   a. Always follow nouns.

   b. All non-human plurals take feminine singular
      adjectives.

   c. Have one plural for feminine and masculine.

TAPE II/SIDE 2

Review Drills

Transform the following into plural.

First repeat the sentence, then change it into plural.

1. da mohandis gidiid   This is a new engineer.
   dool mohandisiin godaad

2. di mowàzzàfà zàriifà   This is a nice employee.
   dool mowàzzàfààt zoràaf

3. da modiir ģáátir   This is a clever manager.
   dool modiriin ģátriin

4. di ģa''a rixiisá   This is a cheap apartment.
   di ģo'a' rixiisá

5. da ba''aal ġaali   This is an expensive grocer.
   dool ba''aliin ġalyiin

6. da ģaariç waasiç   This is a wide street.
   di ģawaariç wasça

7. da bántáloon táwiil   These are long trousers.
   di bántálonáát táwiilá

8. di çárábiyyá amrikaani   This is an American car.
   di çárábiyyáát amrikaani

9. di moģkila mohimma   This is an important
   di maģaakil mohimma   problem.

10. di lokándá kibiira   This is a big hotel.
    di lokándáát kibiira

11. da su'aal sahl   This is an easy question.
    di as'ila sahla

12. da ámiis dayya'   This is a tight shirt.
    di omsáán dayya'a

NOTE:

1. giddan
   xáális
   awi   All three mean "very"

2. "giddan," "xáális" and "awi" will always follow the
   adjective. For example:
   very wide   waasiç giddan
   very tall   táwiil xáális
   very pretty   hilw awi

36

"giddan," xȧȧlis" and "awi"

Answer the Following Questions Affirmatively, Using
"giddan," "xȧȧlis" and "awi," in that Order.

1. ilmodiir ǵȧȧtir?

    aywa, ǵȧȧtir giddan

2. ilbeet waasiç?

    aywa, waasiç xȧȧlis

3. ilbint hilwa?

    aywa, hilwa awi

4. ilmowȧzzȧfiin kwayyisiin?

    aywa, kwayyisiin giddan

5. il'owȧd kibiira?

    aywa, kibiira xȧȧlis

6. ilbawwabiin kaslaniin?

    aywa, kaslaniin awi

7. iǵǵawaariç nidiifȧ?

    aywa, nidiifȧ giddan

TAPE II/SIDE 2

Replacement

Answer the Following Questions Using a Pronoun Instead
of the Subject

    Mona ǵȧtrȧ, miǵ kida?

    aywa, hiyya ǵȧtrȧ

1. Mohamed we Mona zorȧȧf?

    aywa, homma zorȧȧf

2. Nadia ṭåwiilå?
   aywa, hiyya ṭåwiilå
3. Ana we Mona kaslaniin?
   aywa, intu kaslaniin
4. Mohamned gaçaan?
   aywa, howwa gaçaan
5. Mona we Nancy çåṭs̸åniin?
   aywa, homma çåṭs̸åniin

TAPE II/SIDE 2

<u>Translation</u>

<u>Translate the Following Sentences Into Arabic</u>

(Not all sentences are transcribed)

1.	We are hungry.	iḥna gaçaniin
2.	This is a new hotel.	di lokåndå gidiida
3.	These are good employees.	dool mowåẓẓåfiin kwayyisiin
4.	They are tall boys.	homma awlaad ṭowåål
5.	You are a clever girl.	inti bint s̸åṭrå

Owning Things

The Possessive Pronominal Suffix

To express possession in Arabic we add a <u>suffix</u> to the noun:

office	maktab
my office	maktab<u>i</u>
their office	maktab<u>hom</u>

The "i" and the "hom" which we add to the noun "maktab" are what we call <u>possessive pronominal suffixes</u>. These suffixes are a means by which we can express the idea that <u>something belongs to someone</u>. The following section contains a list of these suffixes.

TAPE III/SIDE 1

<u>Suffixes</u>

<u>Please Listen and Repeat</u>

maktab   office/desk

English	Word	Suffix pronoun
my office	maktab	i
your office (m.s.)	maktab	ak
your office (f.s.)	maktab	ik
his office	maktab	u (h)
her office	maktab	ha
our office	maktab	na
your office (pl.)	maktab	ku
their office	maktab	hom

39

Nouns that end in one consonant (C) take the suffixes as they are in the table above. However, this is not the case with nouns that end in two consonants (CC) or nouns that end in a vowel (V) or even the feminine nouns that end in an "a."

We will therefore give you a separate list for:

1. Nouns that end in C
2. Nouns that end in CC
3. Nouns that end in V
4. Feminine Nouns (Group I/II)

Nouns that End in "C"

English	Word	Suffix
house	beet	i
		ak
		ik
book	kitaab	u (h)
manager/boss	modiir	ha
		na
teacher	modarris	ku
		hom

Nouns that End in "CC"

Egyptian Arabic does not allow the sequence CCC. A helping vowel is used when the noun ends in CC and the suffix pronoun begins with a C:

bint	girl, daughter
binti	my girl, my daughter
bint<u>aha</u>	her daughter

The word "<u>bint</u>" ends in CC and the suffix "ha" begins with a C. We need to break the sequence CC-C by using a helping vowel. Here is a list of the pronominal suffixes:

Suffixes

Please Listen and Repeat

¢oġl	work
my work	¢oġl i
your work (m.s.)	¢oġl ak
your work (f.s.)	¢oġl ik
his work	¢oġl u (h)
her work	¢oġl aha
our work	¢oġl ina
your work (pl.)	¢oġl oku
their work	¢oġl ohom

NOTE:

We added a helping vowel where CCC would have occurred. Here are more examples:

Word	English	Suffix
wa't	time	i
ca'd	contract	ak
akl	food	ik
ism	name	u (h)
		aha
		ina
		oku
		ohom

Nouns that End with a "V"

In the section on nouns we talked about a group of nouns that end in a "V":

korsi, mabna, abu

What happens to these nouns when we add a suffix to them? We simply add another vowel to the end of the noun, then we suffix the pronoun. Here is an example:

mabna	building	korsi	chair
mabnaaha	her building	korsiiha	her chair

TAPE III/SIDE 1

Suffixes

Please Listen and Repeat

korsi	chair	
my chair	korsi	yya
your chair	korsi	ik (m.s.)
your chair	korsi	iki (f.s.)
his chair	korsi	ih
her chair	korsi	iha
our chair	korsi	ina
your chair	korsi	iku (pl.)
their chair	korsi	ihom

Notice what happens with the first person singular "korsiyya" and the second person (feminine singular) "korsiiki."

More examples:

Word	English	Suffix
karaasi	chairs	VV y a
mabna	building	VV k
mabaani	buildings	VV k i
abu	father of	VV (h)
axu	brother of	VV ha
		VV ku
		VV hom

42

Nouns Ending With "C"

We will give you a sentence followed by a subject pronoun. Please add the correct pronominal suffix to the noun.

maktab	office
Da maktab miin?	Whose office is this?
ana	da maktab<u>i</u>
I	This is <u>my</u> office.

1. Da maktab miin?

    inta

    da maktabak

    This is <u>your</u> office. (m.s.)

2. Da maktab miin?

    inti

    da maktab<u>ik</u>

    This is <u>your</u> office. (f.s.)

3. Da maktab miin?

    howwa

    da maktabu(h)

    This is <u>his</u> office.

4. Da maktab miin?

    hiyya

    da maktab<u>ha</u>

    This is <u>her</u> office.

5. Da maktab miin?

    ihna

    da maktab<u>na</u>

    This is <u>our</u> office.

6. Da maktab miin?

    intu

    da maktab<u>ku</u>

    This is <u>your</u> office.

7. Da maktab miin?

    homma

    da maktab<u>hom</u>

    This is <u>their</u> office.

åmiis   shirt

1. Da åmiis miin?
    ana   da åmiisi
2. Da åmiis miin?
    inta   da åmiisak
3. Da åmiis miin?
    inti   da åmiisik
4. Da åmiis miin?
    howwa   da åmiisu (h)
5. Da åmiis miin?
    hiyya   da åmisha
6. Da åmiis miin?
    ihna   da åmisna
7. Da åmiis miin?
    intu   da åmisku
8. Da åmiis miin?
    homma   da åmishom

TAPE III/SIDE 1

Ask Questions Using "miʃ kida"

båntåloon   trousers
ana   da båntålooni, miʃ kida?
1. inta   da båntåloonak, miʃ kida?
2. inti   da båntåloonik, miʃ kida?
3. howwa   da båntåloonu(h), miʃ kida?
4. hiyya   da båntåloonha, miʃ kida?
5. ihna   da båntålonna, miʃ kida?
6. intu   da båntålonku, miʃ kida?
7. homma   da båntålonhom, miʃ kida?

44

Respond to the Following Question with "aho."

feen beetak?   Where is your house?

aho beeti   Here is my house.

1.   feen beetik?   aho beeti

2.   feen beetu (h)?   aho beetu(h)

3.   feen betha?   aho betha

4.   feen betna?   aho betna

5.   feen betku?   aho betna

6.   feen bethom?   aho bethom

TAPE III/SIDE 1

Nouns Ending With "CC"

Answer the Following Questions Using the Correct Suffix
Pronoun.

ṣoġl   work

1.   Da ṣoġl miin?
     ana   da ṣoġli

2.   inta   da ṣoġlak

3.   inti   da ṣoġlik

4.   howwa   da ṣoġlu (h)

5.   hiyya   da ṣoġlaha

6.   ihna   da ṣoġlina

7.   intu   da ṣoġloku

8.   homma   da ṣoġlohom

akl   food

1.   Da akl E miin?

2.   inta   da aklak

45

3.	inti	da aklik
4.	howwa	da aklu (h)
5.	hiyya	da akl<u>aha</u>
6.	iḥna	da akl<u>ina</u>
7.	intu	da akl<u>oku</u>
8.	homma	da akl<u>ohom</u>

Ask Questions Using "miʃ kida."

ça'd   contract

1.	ana	da ça'di, miʃ kida?
2.	inta	da ça'dak, miʃ kida?
3.	inti	da ça'dik, miʃ kida?
4.	howwa	da ça'du (h), miʃ kida?
5.	hiyya	da ça'<u>daha</u>, miʃ kida?
6.	iḥna	da ça'd<u>ina</u>, miʃ kida?
7.	intu	da ça'<u>doku</u>, miʃ kida?
8.	homma	da ça'<u>dohom</u>, miʃ kida?

TAPE III/SIDE 1

Nouns Ending with "V"

Respond to the following questions with "aho,"
"ahe," or "ahom," depending on whether the word given
you is singular or plural.

korsi   chair
karaasi   chairs

1.	feen korsiyya?	aho korsiiki
	Where is my chair?	Here's your chair.
2.	feen korsiik?	aho korsiyya

3.	feen karasiiki?	ahe karasiyya
4.	feen korsii(h)?	aho korsii(h)
5.	feen korsiiha	aho korsiiha
6.	feen karasiina?	ahe karasiiku
7.	feen karasiiku	ahe karasiina
8.	feen karasiihom	ahe karasiihom

Respond to the Following Question Using the Correct Suffix:

axu	brother of
Miin da?	Who is this?
Da axuuya	This is my brother.

1.	Miin da?	
	inta	da axuuk
2.	inti	da axuuki
3.	howwa	da axuu (h)
4.	hiyya	da axuuha
5.	ihna	da axuuna
6.	intu	da axuuku
7.	homma	da axuuhom

Ask Questions Using "miş kida"

abu		father of
1.	inta	da abuuk, miş kida?
2.	inti	da abuuki, miş kida?
3.	howwa	da abuuh, miş kida?
4.	hiyya	da abuuha, miş kida?
5.	ihna	da abuuna, miş kida?
6.	intu	da abuuku, miş kida?
7.	homma	da abuuhom, miş kida?

Owning Things (continuation)

Feminine Nouns (Group I/II)

The mark of a feminine singular noun is the feminine ending "a."

gazm<u>a</u>   shoe

ʃánt<u>a</u>   bag

ʃaʼʼ<u>a</u>   apartment

To <u>add</u> a possessive pronominal suffix to a feminine noun as a manner of expressing possession, we must do the following:

1.   The feminine ending "a" is changed into "-it":

gazma   gazmit

ʃántà   ʃántit

2.   After we drop the "a" and add "-it" we suffix the pronoun:

gazma   gazmit

my shoe   gazmit <u>i</u>

ʃántà   ʃántit

my bag   ʃántit <u>i</u>

TAPE III/SIDE 2

Feminine Nouns, Group I

Please Listen and Repeat

ʃaʼʼa   apartment

ʃaʼʼa   ʃaʼʼit

48

English	Word	Suffix
my apartment	ʃa"it	i
your apartment	ʃ"it	ak
your apartment	ʃa"it	ik
his apartment	ʃa"it	u (h)
her apartment	ʃa"it	ha
our apartment	ʃa"it	na
your apartment	ʃa"it	ku
their apartment	ʃa"it	hom

There are two groups of feminine nouns. The words "sa"a", "gazma" and "ʃàntà" belong to Group I.

Examples of Feminine Nouns, Group I

nimra	number
mokalma	telephone call
gomla	sentence
kilma	word
fikra	idea
ʃirka	company

TAPE III/SIDE 2

Feminine Nouns, Group II:

Please Listen and Repeat

oodà	room	
oodà	odt	odti

English	Word	Suffix
my room	odt	i
your room	odt	ak
your room	odt	ik
his room	odt	u (h)
her room	odit	ha
our room	odit	na
your room	odit	ku
their room	odit	hom

REMARKS:

1. We shorten the long vowel throughout:

   oodå   odt

2. We dropped the "i" with the first, second and third person pronouns (except for the third person feminine).

   oodit   odt

3. We replace the "i" with the third person feminine and the first, second and third person plural.

   This happens predominantly to feminine singular nouns which have an internal long vowel. There are other levels of explanation that are more complicated. At this stage we request that you concentrate on the sound of the word.

Examples of Feminine Nouns, Group II

oodå	room
suurå	picture
tåråbeezå	table
sigåårå	cigarette
wallaaça	lighter

ṣaġġaala	maid, servant
saaça	hour, watch, clock
kobbaaya	glass
izaaza	bottle
moṣkila	problem
mas'ala	problem
maktaba	library
maknasa	broom, vacuum cleaner
mànti'à	area, quarter district

The above words follow what we have done to the word "oodà." Please review your rules well before you begin the drills on the tape.

TAPE III/SIDE 2

Feminine Nouns, Group I

Answer the Following Using a Suffix Pronoun

ṣàntà	bag, suitcase
di ṣàntit miin?	
ana	di ṣàniti

1.	inta	di ṣàntitak
2.	inti	di ṣàntitik
3.	howwa	di ṣàntitu (h)
4.	hiyya	di ṣàntitha
5.	ihna	di ṣàntitna
6.	intu	di ṣàntitku
7.	homma	di ṣàntithom

nimra	number
di	nimrit miin?

1.	ana	di nimriti
2.	inta	di nimritak
3.	inti	di nimritik
4.	howwa	di nimritu (h)
5.	hiyya	di nimritha
6.	ihna	di nimritna
7.	intu	di nimritku
8.	homma	di nimrithom

fikra	idea

1.	ana	di fikriti
2.	inta	di fikritak
3.	inti	di fikritik
4.	howwa	di fikritu (h)
5.	hiyya	di fikritha
6.	ihna	di fikritna
7.	intu	di fikritku
8.	homma	di fikrithom

TAPE III/SIDE 2

Feminine Nouns, Group II

Answer the Questions Using a Suffix

oodà	room

1.	ana	di oḍti
2.	inta	di oḍtak
3.	inti	di oḍtik
4.	howwa	di oḍtu (h)
5.	hiyya	di oḍitha
6.	ihna	di oḍitna
7.	intu	di oḍitku
8.	homma	di oḍithom

moʃkila   problem

1.	ana	di moʃkilti
2.	inta	di moʃkiltak
3.	inti	di moʃkiltik
4.	howwa	di moʃkiltu (h)
5.	hiyya	di moʃkilitha
6.	ihna	di moʃkilitna
7.	intu	di moʃkilitku
8.	homma	di moʃkilithom

wallaaça   lighter

di wallaaçit miin?

1.	ihna	di wallaçitna
2.	howwa	di wallaçtu (h)
3.	hiyya	di wallaçitha
4.	ana	di wallaçti
5.	inta	di wallaçtak
6.	inti	di wallaçtik
7.	homma	di wallaçithom

TAPE III/SIDE 2

Review Drill

Translation from English into Arabic

(No transcriptions)

More Ways of Expressing Ownership

The Construct

The construct "idaafa" is another way of expressing possession. The construct is the equivalent of the English "something of something." Here is an example:

The house of Mohamed.   beet Mohamed

What are the components of a construct?

1.   We need two nouns to express "----- of -----."

2.   When the two nouns are indefinite, i.e., when neither has the article "il," then we have an indefinite construct.

       a director of an office   modiir maktab

       a door of a house   baab beet

       a contract of a company   ça'd çirka

3.   When the second noun is definite we have a definite construct.

       the director of the office   modiir ilmaktab

       the door of the house   baab ilbeet

       the contract of the company ça'd içirka

NOTE:

1.   The formula can be:

       noun + noun   OR   noun + ilnoun

2.   In the definite construct, the first noun never

55

takes "il." <u>Only</u> the <u>second</u> noun takes "il." This makes the whole construct definite.

3.   NEVER confuse a construct with a noun adjective phrase.

construct	modiir ilmaktab
noun adjective phrase	<u>il</u>modiir <u>ig</u>gidiid

Adjectives agree with nouns.
Constructs express "----- of -----."

Construct with Nouns ending in C/ CC/ V:

Add the second noun to the first to obtain "----- of -----."

beet Mohamed	house of Mohemed
bàntàloon ilwalad	trousers of the boy
maktab iṣṣirka	office of the company
ṣoġl Mona	the work of Mona
akl Mohamed	the food of Mohamed
korsi ilmaktab	the chair of the desk
tarzi Mohamed	the tailor of Mohamed

Constructs with Feminine Nouns (Group I/II):

All the rules we have presented thus far in the section on possessive pronominal suffixes with feminine nouns (Group I/II) apply here:

Feminine Nouns Group I

ṣàntà	bag
ṣàntit Samia	bag of Samia

56

Feminine Nouns Group II

moʃkila   problem

moʃkilt iʃʃàrq il'àwsàt   problem of the <u>Middle
                                           East</u>

TAPE IV/SIDE 1

The Construct

Translate the Following by Using a Construct.

the office of Mohamed   maktab Mohamed

1.   the office of the director   maktab ilmodiir
2.   the house of Mona   beet Mona
3.   the chair of the desk   korsi lmaktab
4.   the daughter of the manager   bint ilmodiir
5.   the company of the
        telephones   ʃirkit ittilifonaat
6.   the door of the house   baab ilbeet
7.   the street of the house   ʃaariç ilbeet
8.   the house of the girl   beet ilbint
9.   the number of the telephone   nimrit ittilifoon
10. the glass of Mona   kobbaayit Mona

Answer the Following Questions Using a Construct Instead of a Suffix Pronoun.

Da beetak?   la', da beet ilmodiir

Is this your house?   No, this is the house of the
                                 manager.

1.   da beetik?

      (Mona)   la' da beet Mona

2. di nimritak?

(Mohamed)   la' di nimrit Mohamed

3. di moʃkilitha?

(iʃʃirka)   la', di moʃkilt iʃʃirka

4. di wallaçtu (h)

(ilmodiir)   la', di wallaçt ilmodiir

5. di ʃa"itna?

(Samia we Mohamed)   la', di ʃa"it Samia we Mohamed

6. di gazmithom?

(ilbint)   la', di gazmit ilbint

7. da korsiik?

(abuuya)   la', da korsi abuuya

8. di fikritku?

(ilmowȧzzȧfiin)   la', di fikrit ilmowȧzzȧfiin

9. di odtik?

(axuuha)   la', di oodit axuuha

10. da ostazku?

(Mohamed)   la', da ostaaz Mohamed

TAPE IV/SIDE 1

Formation of Sentences

Form constructs from the two sets of words we will give
you, then ask a question using "miʃ kida."

nimra   Samia

di nimrit Samia, miʃ kida?

1. tilifoon   Mohamed

   da tilifoon Mohamed, miʃ kida?

58

2. ȼa"a   Nadia

    di ȼa"it Nadia, miȼ kida?

3. ostaaz   ȼàràbi

    da ostaaz ȼarabi, miȼ kida?

4. ostaaza   ȼàràbi

    di ostaazit ȼàràbi, miȼ kida?

5. korsi   maktab

    da korsi maktab, miȼ kida?

6. moȼkila   Mona

    di moȼkilit Mona, miȼ kida?

7. kobbaaya   laban (milk)

    di kobbaayit laban, miȼ kida?

8. izaaza   mayya (water)

    di ȼzaazit màyyà, miȼ kida?

9. mowàzzàfiin   iȼȼirka

    dool mowàzzàfiin iȼȼirka, miȼ kida?

10. madrasa (school)   il'awlaad (children)

    di madrast il'awlaad, miȼ kida?

"Bitaaȼ," Bitaaȼa" and "Bituuȼ"

There are two ways to express belonging or
possession. One is by using <u>possessive</u> <u>pronominal</u>
<u>suffixes</u>. The other is by using <u>constructs</u>. In this
section we will present you with a <u>third</u> way of
expressing possession which is particular to spoken
Egyptian. We have already seen:

beetu (h)   his house
beet Mohamed   the house of Mohamed.

Now we will add:

ilbeet <u>bitaaȼ</u> Mohamed
the house that belongs to Mohamed.

"Bitaaç," "bitaaça" and "bituuç" are also means of expressing belonging. However, their use is restricted to certain cases.

1. "Bitaaç": is the singular masculine form. It is used with singular masculine nouns. It always agrees with the noun that preceeds it in gender and number.

    maktab   ilmaktab bitaaç ilmodiir

2. "Bitaaça": is the singular feminine form. It is used with singular feminine words and non-human plurals. It always agrees with the noun that preceeds it. "Bitaaça" has the feminine ending "a." It belongs to the same category as the feminine nouns of Group II. The rules we applied to them apply here.

    ṣàntà   ----- bitaaça ----- Samia

    The bag that belongs to Samia.

    iṣṣàntà bitaaçit Samia

    NOTE: We transformed the "a" at the end of "bitaaça" to "-it."

3. "Bituuç": is the plural form for both masculine and feminine. It is used with human plurals. It always agrees with the noun that preceeds it.

    mowàzzàfiin   iṣṣirka

    ilmowàzzàfiin bituuç iṣṣirka

    The employees of the company

60

"Bitaaç," bitaaça," and "bituuç" take the suffix pronouns:

ɣoġl   work

ɣoġli   iɣɣoġl bitaaçi
ɣoġlak   iɣɣoġl bitaaçak
ɣoġlik   iɣɣoġl bitaaçik

ɣàntà   bag

ɣàntitik   iɣɣàntà bitaaçtik
ɣàntitna   iɣɣàntà bitaçitna
ɣàntithom   iɣɣàntà bitaçithom

mowàzzàfiin   employees

mowàzzàfiinak   ilmowàzzàfiin bituuçak
mowàzzàfiinu (h)   ilmowàzzàfiin bituuçu (h)

Use of "Bitaaç"

"Bitaaç" is Used:

1. In relationships between human beings and things.

2. In business relationships:

    ba"aal   grocer
    my grocer   ilba"aal bitaaçi

    mohaami   lawyer
    my lawyer   ilmohaami bitaaçi

modiir   boss, manager

my boss   ilmodiir bitaaçi

xȧyyȧȧtȧ   dressmaker

my dressmaker   ilxȧyyȧȧtȧ bitaçti

NOTE: NEVER use "bitaaç" to establish <u>family</u>
         <u>relations</u> (father, mother, etc.) or <u>human</u>
         <u>realtions</u> (friends, neighbors, etc.).

TAPE IV/SIDE 1

<u>Transformation</u>

<u>Use "bitaaç," "bitaaça," or "bituuç," to Transform the</u>
<u>Following.</u>

maktabi   waasiç
ilmaktab bitaaçi waasiç

1.   maktabha <u>waasiç</u>   Her office is <u>spacious</u>.
     il maktab bitaçha waasiç

2.   maktabku waasiç
     ilmaktab bitaçku waasiç

3.   modiiri ¢ȧȧtir   My boss is <u>clever</u>.
     il modiir bitaaçi ¢ȧȧtir

4.   modiirak ¢ȧȧtir
     ilmodiir bitaaçak ¢ȧȧtir

5.   modirna ¢ȧȧtir
     ilmodiir bitaçna ¢ȧȧtir

6.   korsiih <u>adiim</u>   His chair is <u>old</u>.
     ilkorsi bitaaçu (h) adiim

62

7. korsiiha adiim

   ikkorsi bitaçha adiim

8. korsiina adiim

   ikkorsi bitaçna adiim

9. korsiiku gidiid

   ikkorsi bitaçku gidiid

10. ŝántiti gidiida

    iŝŝántà bitaçti gidiida

11. ŝántithom gidiida

    iŝŝántà bitaçithom gidiida

12. ba"aalak ġaali   Your grocer is <u>expensive</u>.

    ilba"aal bitaçaak ġaali

13. ba"aalik ġaali

    ilba"aal bitaaçik ġaali

14. ŝaġġalitna <u>kwayyisa</u>   Our maid is <u>good</u>.

    iŝŝaġġaala bitaçitna kwayyisa

15. ŝaġġalithom kwayyisa

    iŝŝaġġaala bitaçithom kwayyisa

TAPE IV/SIDE 1

Review Drills

Transform the Following into Constructs Then Translate
Them:

ilmaktab bitaaç Mohamed

maktab Mohamed

1. ilmaktab bitaaç ilmodiir

   maktab ilmodiir   the manager's office

2. ikkorsi bitaaç ilmaktab

   korsi lmaktab   the desk chair

63

3. ittilifoon bitaaç ilbeet
   tilifoon ilbeet   the home telephone

4. innimra bitaaçit Samia
   nimrit Samia   Samia's number

5. ilmoʃkila bitaçt ilmàyyà
   moʃkilt ilmàyyà   the water problem

6. ilfikra bitaçt iʃʃirka
   fikrit iʃʃirka   the company's idea

7. ilçàràbiyyà bitaçt ilwaziir
   çàràbiyyit ilwaziir   the minister's car

8. il'ostaaza bitaçt ilçàràbi
   ostazt ilçarbi   the professor of Arabic

9. iʃʃa"a bitaaçit Nadia
   ʃa"it Nadia   Nadia's apartment

10. iʃʃariç bitaaç ilmaktab
    ʃaariç ilmaktab   the office street

Locating Things and Places

In this section we will deal with <u>prepositions</u> and <u>prepositions with pronominal suffixes</u>.

TAPE IV/SIDE 2

<u>List of Prepositions</u>

<u>Please Listen and Repeat</u>.

foo'	on top of ..., upstairs
oddaam	in front of ...
fi	in
li	for
çaŝaan	for
bi	with
bàrrà	outside
gowwa	inside
wayya	with
wàrà	behind
maça	with
taht	under, downstairs
abl	before
baçd	after
gamb	near, beside
çand	at (the French "chez"), to have
min	from

The Prepositions

Translate the Following:

1. The street is in front of the house.

    iṣṣaariҁ oddaam ilbeet

2. The car is beside the house.

    ilҁàràbiyyà gamb ilbeet

3. My car is behind their house.

    ҁàràbiyyiti wàrà bethom

4. The manager is in his office.

    ilmodiir fi maktabu (h)

5. The girl is in her room.

    il bint fi oditha

6. The bag is on the chair.

    iṣṣànta ҁala kkorsi

7. Their street is before our house.

    ṣaariҁhom abl betna

8. Mohamed is at Mona's.

    Mohamed ҁand Mona

9. The hotel is outside Cairo.

    illokàndà bàrrà lqààhirà

10. The glass is with Nadia.

    ikkobbaaya maҁa Nadia

Prepositions and Suffix Pronouns

    Arabic prepositions take suffix pronouns as
objects, i.e., instead of using a noun as an object, we
use a pronoun and add it to the preposition as a suffix.
Here are some examples:

1.　innimra çand Mohamed

　　The number is with Mohamed.

　　innimra çandu (h)

　　The number is with him.

2.　innimra çand ilbint

　　innimra çandaha

　　The number is with her.

3.　innimra çand Mohamed we Nancy

　　innimra çandohom

　　The number is with them.

Sentences of this type answer questions such as "with whom?" "behind whom?" "before whom?" depending on the preposition used.

How do we suffix the object pronouns to the prepositions? The rules we applied to nouns ending in C/ CC/ V apply here. Some prepositions end in one C "foo'," others end in CC "abl," "gamb" and others end in V "maça," "fi," "wara." Here are some examples:

TAPE IV/SIDE 2

Prepositions ending in C "foo'":

foo'	i
foo'	ak
foo'	ik
foo'	u (h)
fo'	ha
fo'	na
fo'	ku
fo'	hom

Prepositions ending in CC "gamb":

gamb	i
gamb	ak
gamb	ik
gamb	u (h)
gamb	aha
gamb	ina
gamb	oku
gamb	ohom

Prepositions ending in V "maça":

maça	aya
maça	ak
maça	aki
maça	a(h)
maça	aha
maça	ana
maça	aku
maça	ahom

Prepositions with Suffix Pronouns

foo' (on top)	'oddaam (in front)	li (for)
foo'i	oddaami	liyya
foo'ak	oddaamak	liik
foo'ik	oddaamik	liiki
foo'u (h)	oddaamu	liih
fo'ha	oddamha	liiha
fo'na	oddamna	liina
fo'ku	oddamku	liiku
fo'hom	oddamhom	liihom

wara (behind)	maça (with)	wayya (with)
wàràaya	maçaaya	wayyaaya
wàràak	maçaak	wayyaak
wàràaki	maçaaki	wayyaaki
wàràah	maçaah	wayyaah
wàràahà	maçaaha	wayyaaha
wàràana	maçaana	wayyaana
wàràaku	maçaaku	wayyaaku
wàràahom	maçaahom	wayyaahom

taht (under)	'abl (before)	baçd (after)
tahti	abli	baçdi
tahtak	ablak	baçdak
tahtik	ablik	baçdik
tahtu(h)	ablu (h)	baçdu (h)
tahtaha	ablaha	baçdaha
tahtina	ablina	baçdina
tahtoku	abluku	baçdoku
tahtohom	ablohom	baçdohom

gamb (beside)	çand (to have at/"chez")	min (from)
gambi	çandi	minni
gambak	çandak	minnak
gambik	çandik	minnik
gambu (h)	çandu (h)	minnu (h)
gambaha	çandaha	minnaha
gambina	çandina	minnina
gamboku	çandoku	minnoku
gambohom	çandohom	minnohom

TAPE IV/SIDE 2

Prepositions with Suffixes

Add the Suffix Pronoun to the Preposition:

The money is with me

ilfoluus maça   (ana)

ilfoluus maçaaya

1. ilfoluus maça (inta)

    ilfoluus maçaak

2. ilfoluus maça (inti)

    ilfoluus maçaaki

3. ilfoluus maça (howwa)

    ilfoluus maçaa (h)

4. ilfoluus maça (hiyya)

    ilfoluus maçaaha

5. ilfoluus maça (ihna)

    ilfoluus maçaana

6. ilfoluus maça (intu)

    ilfoluus maçaaku

7. ilfoluus maça (homma)

    ilfoluus maçaahom

Answer the Following Using a Suffix Pronoun:

Samia feen?   Where is Samia?

Samia wàràáya   Samia is behind me.

1. Mohamed feen?

    Mohamed wàrà (inta)

    Mohamed wàràak

2. Mohamed wårå (inti)

   Mohamed wåråaki

3. Mohamed wårå (howwa)

   Mohamed wåråa (h)

4. Mohamed wårå (hiyya)

   Mohamed wåråaha

5. Mohamed wårå (ihna)

   Mohamed wåråana

6. Mohamed wårå (intu)

   Mohamed wåråaku

7. Mohamed wårå (homma)

   Mohamed wåråahom

"çand"   "to have"

Egyptian Arabic expresses "to have" through the preposition "çand." Once we add a suffix pronoun to "çand" we obtain "I have," "you have," etc. Here are some examples.

TAPE IV/SIDE 2

Please Listen and Repeat

I have a car.	çandi çåråbiyyå
You have a car.	çandak çåråbiyyå
You have a car.	çanik çåråbiyyå
He has a car.	çandu (h) çåråbiyyå
She has a car.	çandaha çåråbiyyå
We have a car.	çandina çåråbiyyå
You have a car.	çandoku çåråbiyyå
They have a car.	çandohom çåråbiyyå

When "çand" means "to have" it occurs <u>at the</u> <u>beginning of the sentence</u>. Otherwise, "<u>çand</u>" means "with" or "at someone's house/place."

TAPE IV/SIDE 2

<u>Answer the Following by Using a Suffix Pronoun</u>

ilça'd çand miin?
The contract is with whom?   (who has the contract)
ilça'd çand (ana)
    ilça'd çandi

1.   ilça'd çand (inta)
    ilça'd çandak

2.   ilça'd çand (howwa)
    ilça'd çandu (h)

3.   ilça'd çand (hiyya)
    ilça'd çandaha

4.   ilça'd çand (ihna)
    ilça'd çandina'

5.   ilça'd çand (intu)
    ilça'd çandoku

6.   ilça'd çand (homma)
    ilça'd çandohom

<u>iggawaab</u> da <u>limiin</u>?   This <u>letter</u> is for whom?
iggawaab da li (ana)
iggawwab da liyya

1. iggawaab da li (inta)

   iggawaab da liik

2. iggawaab da li (inti)

   iggawaab da liiki

3. iggawaab da li (howwa)

   iggawaab da lii (h)

4. iggawaab da li (hiyya)

   iggawaab da liiha

5. iggawaab da li (ihna)

   iggawaab da liina

6. iggawaab da li (intu)

   iggawaab da liiku

7. iggawaab da li (homma)

   iggawaab da liihom

TAPE IV/SIDE 2

Substitute the Object with a Pronominal Suffix

1. da çaɣaan ilmodiir   da çaɣaanu (h)
2. ilfoluus wayya Samia   ilfoluus wayyaaha
3. ilçàràbiyyà wàrà llikàndà   ilçàràbiyyà wàrààhà
4. ilwallaaça maça rràagil   ilwallaaça maçaah
5. ikkorsi gamb ilbint   ikkorsi gambaha
6. ilçàràbiyyà maça l'awlaad   ilçàràbiyyà maçaahom

Answer the Following Questions:

1. ilmoftaah maçaaku?   aywa ilmoftaah maçaana
2. ilmoftaah maçaak?   aywa ilmoftaah maçaaya
3. waraaku ɣoġl?   aywa, wàrààna ɣoġl

73

4. waraaki ɟogl?   aywa, wàràáya ɟogl
5. iɟɟántà gambak?   aywa, iɟɟántà gambi
6. iɟɟántà gambuku?   aywa, iɟɟántà gambuku
7. iggawaab minnak?   aywa, iggawaab minni

Counting/Telling Time

The Numbers

TAPE V/SIDE 1

Numbers

Please Listen and Repeat

one	waahid	eleven	hidaaşar
two	itneen	twelve	itnaaşar
three	talaata	thirteen	talataaşar
four	arbaça	fourteen	arbaçtaaşar
five	xamsa	fifteen	xamstaaşar
six	sitta	sixteen	sittaaşar
seven	sabça	seventeen	sabaçtaaşar
eight	tamania	eighteen	tamantaaşar
nine	tisça	nineteen	tisaçtaaşar
ten	çaşarà	twenty	çişriin

twenty-one	waahid we çişriin
twenty-two	itneen we çişriin
twenty-three	talaata w çişriin
thirty-one	waahid we talatiin
thirty-two	itneen we talatiin
thirty-nine	tisça wtalatiin
forty	arbiçiin
fifty	xamsiin

75

sixty	sittiin
seventy	sabҫiin
eighty	tamaniin
ninety	tisҫiin
one hundred	miyya
two hundred	miteen
three hundred	toltomiyya
four hundred	robҫomiyya
five hundred	xomsomiyya
one thousand	alf
two thousand	alfeen

Numbers From Three to Ten

1. If the number appears <u>alone</u>, i.e., if it is not followed by a noun, then it will take its complete form:

   ҫandak <u>kaam</u> ҫàràbiyyà?

   <u>How many</u> cars do you have?

   kaam   how many

   ҫandi talaata

   I have three.

   ҫandi xamsa

   I have five.

2. After <u>kaam</u> we always have a <u>singular</u> noun:

   ҫandak kaam <u>badla</u>?

   How many suits do you have?

   ҫandik kaam <u>gazma</u>?

   How many shoes do you have?

   Questions are formed by using "<u>kaam</u>" and singular

3. In answering the question:

çandak kaam badla?

the number will be followed by a plural noun (i.e., numbers from three to ten). Here is an example:

çandi xamas bidal

I have five suits.

4. When numbers from three to ten are followed by a noun, they will always appear in their short form. Here are some contrastive examples:

çandak kaam badla?

çandi talaata (complete form)

çandi talat bidal (short form and pl. noun)

çandik kaam gazam?

çandi xamsa

çandi xamas gizam

TAPE V/SIDE 1

Short and Long Forms of the Numbers

Please Listen and Repeat

talaata	talat
àrbàçà	àrbàç
xamsa	xamas
sitta	sitt
sabça	sabaç
tamania	taman
tisça	tisaç
çàṣàrà	çàṣàr

Numbers From Eleven On

1. Starting with <u>eleven</u>, all numbers are followed by a
    <u>singular noun</u>.

     çandak kaam <u>badla</u>?

    çandi hidàȧśȧr badla

2. The number 100 "<u>miyya</u>" appears in that form when
    alone. It takes the form "<u>miit</u>" when followed by
    a noun.

    çandak kaam <u>gineeh</u>?

    How many <u>pounds</u> do you have?

    çandi <u>miyya</u>

    çandi <u>miit</u> gineeh

The Number One

1. The number one has two forms:

    masculine   waahid

    feminine   wahda

2. "One" agrees with the noun in <u>gender</u>:

    çandak kaam <u>walad</u>?

    How many <u>boys</u> do you have?

    çandi walad <u>waahid</u> (m.)

    I have one boy.

    çandak kaam <u>bint</u>?

    How many <u>daughters</u> do you have?

    çandi bint <u>wahda</u> (f.)

3. Unlike numbers from three to ten, number "<u>one</u>"
    <u>follows</u> the noun.

4. Number "<u>one</u>" will take a singular noun.

<u>NOTE:</u>

<u>Never</u> put "<u>waahid</u> or "<u>wahda</u>" before the noun. It will change the meaning of the sentence. For example:

çandi waahid walad fi lmaktab

I have <u>a</u> boy in the office.

çandi walad waahid fi lmaktab

I have <u>one</u> boy in the office.

The Dual

1. We form the dual in Arabic by adding the suffix "<u>-een</u>" to the noun.

   çandak kaam walad?

   çandi walad<u>een</u>.

   I have two sons.

   çandak kaam bint?

   çandi bint<u>een</u>

   I have two daughters.

2. If the noun is feminine, the feminine ending "a" will be changed to "-it," then we will add the suffix "-een."

   çandak kaam ʃa"a?

   How many apartments do you have?

   çandi ʃa"iteen.

   çandak kaam <u>fikra</u>?

   How many ideas do you have?

   çandi <u>fikriteen</u>.

3. Some nouns cannot take the suffix "-een" to form a dual. In these cases the number two "<u>itneen</u>" is

used and is <u>followed</u> by a <u>noun</u> in the <u>plural</u>.   For
example:

"<u>fiih</u>"   there is, there are.

<u>fiih</u> kaam mowȧzzȧf fi ȿȿirka?

How many employees <u>are there</u> in the company?

fiih <u>itneen</u> mowȧzzȧfiin

There are two employees.

4.   It is predominantly <u>human plurals</u> that do not form
      duals. They, therefore, take the number two in
      front of them:

	ba"aliin	two grocers.
itneen	sawwa'iin	two drivers.
	modarrisiin	two teachers.

TAPE V/SIDE 1

<u>Numbers</u>

<u>Answer the Following Questions</u>.

You will answer once with the number alone and once
with the number followed by a noun:

        maçaad   mawaçiid

wȧrȧȧk kaam <u>maçaad</u>?

How many appointments do you have?

maçaad

wȧrȧȧyȧ   3

wȧrȧȧyȧ talaata

wȧrȧȧyȧ talat mawaçiid.

Now begin:

1. wàràáhà kaam maçaad?

   wàràáhà 4

2. wàràáku kaam maçaad?

   wàràáná 5

3. wàràáhom kaam maçaad?

   wàràáhom 1

4. wàràáh kaam maçaad?

   wàràáh 2

5. wàràáki kaam maçaad?

   wàràáyà 6

6. wàràák kaam maçaad?

   wàràáyà 8

TAPE V/SIDE 1

Numbers

Answer the Following

        alam   ilaam

1. çandak kaam <u>alam</u>?

   How many pens do you have?

   çandi xamsa, çandi xamas <u>ilaam</u>.

   I have five, I have five pens.

howwa (6)	çandu (h) sitta, çandu (h) sitt ilaam
hiyya (2)	çandaha tneen, çandaha alam<u>een</u>
ihna (3)	çandina talaata, çandina talat ilaam
homma (9)	çandohom tisça, çandohom tisaç ilaam

81

inta (10)   çandi çàṣàrà, çandi çàṣàr ilaam

<u>sekerteera</u>   <u>sekerteraat</u> (pl.)

2.   Fiih kaam <u>sekerteera</u> fiṣṣirka?

How many <u>secretaries</u> are there in the company?

Fiih talaata, fiih talat sekerteraat

There are three, there are three secretaries.

fiih 5

fiih 1

fiih 9

fiih 4

fiih 2   fiih itneen sekerteraat fiṣṣirka.

TAPE V/SIDE 1

<u>Numbers</u>

<u>Answer the Following</u>

saaça   saçaat

1.   oddaamak ṣoġl kaam saaça?

How many hours of work do you have ahead of you?

oddaami ṣoġl (2)   oddaami soġl sa<u>çteen</u>

oddaamu(h) ṣoġl kaam saaça?

oddaamu(h) ṣoġl (3) talat saçaat

oddamha ṣoġl kaam saaça?

oddamha (1)   saaça <u>wahda</u>

oddamku ṣoġl kaam saaça?

oddamna ṣoġl (5)   xamas saçaat

2. çaleek foluus <u>add eeh</u>?

<u>How much</u> money do you owe?

çalayya árbàçà gneeh

I owe four pounds.

çaleeha føluus add eeh?

çaleeha (2)   çaleeha ítneen gineeh

çaleeku føluus add eeh?

çaleena (8)   çaleena tamania gneeh

çaleeh foluus add eeh?

çaleeh (10)   çaleeh çàɟàrà gneeh

çaleeki foluus add eeh?

çalayyà (5)   çalayya xamsa gneeh

çalayya flous add eeh?

çaleeki (1)   çaleeki gineeh

　　　walad　　　　　　　　awlaad

3. çandu(h) kaam walad?

çandu(h) (12)　çandu(h) itnàà∮àr <u>walad</u>

çandaha kaam walad?

çandaha (15)　　çandaha xamastàà∮àr walad

　　　sana　　　　　　　　siniin

4. çandak kaam sana?

How old are you?

çandi (25)　　　çandi xamsa wçi∮riin sana

çandaha kaam sana?

çandaha (30)　　çandaha talatiin sana

Telling Time

Please Listen and Repeat

issaça kaam <u>min fȧdlȧk?</u>   (m.)

issaça kaam <u>miin fȧdlik?</u>   (f.)

What time is it <u>please?</u>

1.   It is 12:00 <u>noon.</u>

    issaaça itnȧȧ$ȧr <u>iddohr</u>

2.   It is <u>approximately</u> 12:00 noon.

    issaaça itnȧȧ$ȧr iddohr <u>ta'riiban</u>

    issaaça <u>hawaali</u> itnȧȧ$ȧr iddohr

3.   It is one o'clock.

    issaaça wahda

4.   It is 2:05.

    issaça itneen <u>we</u> xamsa   (and)   (plus)

5.   It is 3:10.

    issaaça talaata we ça$ȧrȧ

6.   It is 4:15.

    issaaça ȧrbȧçȧ we <u>robç</u>   (quarter)

7.   It is 5:20.

    issaaça xamsa we <u>tilt</u>   (one third)

8.   It is 6:25.

    issaaça sitta we xamsa wçi$riin <u>di'ii'a.</u>   (minute)

9.   It is 7:30.

    issaaça sabça we <u>noss</u>   (half)

10.   It is 8:35.

    issaça tamania we noss we xamsa

11.   It is 9:40.

    issaaça <u>ça$ȧrȧ</u> <u>illa</u> <u>tilt</u>   (It is <u>ten</u> <u>minus</u> <u>one</u>
                                  <u>third</u>).

12. It is 10:45.

issaaça hidåå$år illa robç

(It is eleven minus one quarter).

13. It is 11:50.

issaaça itnåå$år illa çå$årà

(It is twelve minus ten minutes).

14. It is 11:55 p.m.

issaça ítnåå$år illa xamsa masaa'an

(It is twelve minus five).

15. It is 12:00 exactly.

issaaça ítnåå$år bizzàbt

TAPE V/SIDE 1

Translate the Following

1. It is 11:00 exactly.
2. It is 1:45.
3. It is 2:40.
4. It is 3:30.
5. It is 1:30.
6. It is 12:15.
7. It is 11:45.
8. It is 4:10.
9. It is 6:25.
10. It is 7:05.
11. It is 8:55.
12. It is 9:00 exactly.
13. It is approximately 2.
14. It is approximately 12 p.m.
15. It is 7:15.
16. It is 6:30.
17. It is 5:25.
18. It is 4:05.
19. It is 10:35.
20. It is 9:55.

Buying Things

I Want This

Please Listen and Repeat

1. çaawiz kiilo koosa min fȧdlȧk
   I want one kg. of zuccini please.
2. bikaam?
   How much does it cost?
3. da kitiir awi!
   This is a lot, too much.
4. da ġaali awi!
   This is too expensive.
5. da rixiis awi
   This is very cheap.

1. sȧbȧȧh ilxiir
   Good morning.
2. sȧbȧȧh innuur
   Good morning.
3. çawza itneen kiilo lahma min fȧdlȧk
   I want two kg. of meat please.
4. bikaam ikkiilo?
   How much is the kilo?
5. ikkiilo bi xamsa geneeh

The kilo is LE.5.

6. da ġaali giddan

    This is very expensive.

1. ça̱wziin oodá̱ min fá̱dlá̱k

    We want a room please.

2. bikaam illeela fillokándá̱?

    How much is a night in the hotel?

3. illeela bi xamsiin geneeh

    The night is for LE.50.

4. da rixii̱s giddan

    This is very cheap.

5. il oodá̱ kwayyisa xá̱á̱lis

    The room is very good.

TAPE V/SIDE 2

Please Listen and Repeat

1. ana çaawiz má̱yyá̱ min fá̱dlá̱k

    I want water please.

2. Inta çaawiz ilhi̱saab?

    Do you want the bill?   (cheque)

3. howwa çaawiz ahwa

    He wants coffee.

4. ana çawza ẓaay

    I want tea.

5. inti çawza haa̱ga?

    Do you want something?

6. hiyya çawza <u>foluus</u>
   She wants <u>money</u>.

7. ihna çawziin <u>akl</u>
   We want food.

8. homma çawzin <u>oodà</u>
   They want a <u>room</u>.

TAPE V/SIDE 2

<u>Translate the Following</u>:

1. What time is it?
   It is twelve o'clock exactly.

2. How much does the meat cost?
   The meat costs four pounds.

3. She wants a new car.

4. They want their money.

5. He has one car.

6. I have a house and I want an apartment.

7. Good morning, it is 5:00.

8. We want tea and she wants coffee.

9. I want a hotel outside Cairo.

10. They want a glass of water, please.

TAPE V/SIDE 2

Review Drill

Translate each sentence from Arabic into English.
Change the pronoun from "howwa" into "hiyya" then "ana"
and make all the necessary changes. Here is an example:

çandu (h) akl filtallaaga

He has food in the fridge.

çandaha akl filtallaaga.

çandi akl filtallaga.

Now Begin:

(On tape--no transcriptions)

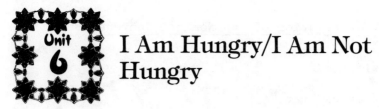

I Am Hungry/I Am Not Hungry

The Nominal Sentence

The nominal sentence can be highly elaborate and, indeed, enables you to say a lot. All you have seen so far are variations on the nominal sentence. Here are some examples:

1. ana Mohamed

    I am Mohamed.

2. howwa amrikaani

    He is American.

3. ihna fi lbeet

    We are at home.

4. hiyya fi lmaktab

    She is in the office.

5. ilmaktab gamb illokåndå

    The office is near the hotel.

6. çandi xamsa weçiʃriin sana

    I am (literally, I have) twenty five years old.

7. fiih ba"aal gamb ilbeet

    There is a grocer near the house.

8. modiir ilmaktab çandu(h) oodå kibiira

    The manager of the office has a big room.

None of the Arabic sentences has a verb in it. That is why we call them nominal sentences.

Negation of the Nominal Sentence

I.   miş:

1.   miş means "not."

2.   It is placed in front of the word it is negating or in the closest position to it.

3.   Miş is the means by which we negate most of the nominal sentences we have seen:

ilmodiir mawguud?

Is the manager present?

la', ilmodiir miş mawguud?

No, the manager is not (present) here.

intu fi lbeet?

Are you at home?

la', ihna miş fi lbeet.

No, we are not at home.

TAPE VI/SIDE 1

Negation of the Nominal Sentence

Negate the Following Sentences Using "miş":

1.   ilmodiir filmaktab

The manager is in the office.

il modiir miş filmaktab

2. ana <u>mawguud</u> filbeet

   I am (present) at home.

   ana mi$ mawguud filbeet

3. mohamed mawguud

   Mohamed is (present) here.

   mohamed mi$ mawguud

4. ilmadrasa kibiira

   The school is big.

   ilmadrasa mi$ kibiira

5. i$$aariç waasiç

   The street is wide.

   i$$aariç mi$ waasiç

6. da beeti

   This is my house.

   da mi$ beeti

7. dool amrikaan

   They are American.

   dool mi$ amrikaan

8. il'akl kwayyis

   The food is good.

   il'akl mi$ kwayyis

9. ilçàràbiyyà gamb ilbeet

   The car is near the house.

   ilçàràbiyyà mi$ gamb ilbeet

10. <u>il'alam</u> taht ikkorsi

    The <u>pen</u> is under the chair.

    il'alam mi$ taht ikkorsi

Answer in the Negative Using "mi$":

1. ilwallaaça di btaçtak?

   Is this lighter yours?

   la' ilwallaaça di mi$ bitaçti

   No, this lighter is not mine.

2. di wallaçtak?

   Is this your lighter?

   la' di mi$ wallaçti

   No, this is not my lighter.

3. ilçàràbiyyà di btaçitha?

   Is this car hers?

   la' ilçàràbiyyà di mi$ bitaçitha

   No this car is not hers.

4. di çàràbiyyithà?

   Is this her car?

   la' di mi$ çàràbiyyitha

   No, this is not her car.

5. da lmodiir bitaçku?

   Is this your boss?

   la' da mi$ lmodiir bitaçna

   No, this is not our boss.

II. Another way we can negate is (la...wala) (neither...nor). For example:

Mohamed filmaktab wala filbeet?

Is Mohamed in the office or at home?

Mohamed la filmaktab, wala filbeet, howwa fillokàndà

Mohamed is neither in the office nor at home, he is in the hotel.

1. "walla" (or) is used in questions only. In order to say "this or that" in a statement use "aw."

He is at the office or at home.
howwa filmaktab aw filbeet.

2. "la/wala" negates two possibilities and affirms a
   third. See example above.

Negation of the Nominal Sentence

Negate, Following This Model

di wallaçtak walla wallaçitha?
di la wallaçti wala wallaçitha, di wallaçtu(h)

1. di çåråbiyyitak walla çåråbiyyitha?
   di la çåråbiyyiti wala çåråbiyyitha, di
   çåråbiyyitu(h)
2. da beetak walla betha?
   da la beeti wala betha, da beetu(h)
3. Di kkobbaaya btaçtak, walla kkobbaaya btaçitha?
   di la kkobbaaya btaçti, wala kkobbaya btaçitha, di
   kkobbaaya btaçtu(h)
4. di kotobak (your books) walla kotobha?
   di la kotobi wala kotobha, di kotobu(h)
5. di nimritak walla nimritha?
   di la nimriti wala nimritha, di nimritu(h)

III. "ma _____ ʃ":

1. "ma _____ ʃ" is originally "miʃ" only it is split
   in two halves so that it surrounds the word it is
   negating rather than preceeds it.

2. We use "ma _____ ʃ" instead of "miʃ" ;with "fiih"
    sentences, i.e., "there is, there are."

    fiih korsi fil'oodà
    There is a chair in the room.

    fiih karaasi fil'oodà
    There are chairs in the room.

    There is a difference between "fi" and "fiih."
"Fi" is a preposition that means "in." "Fiih" is
particular to Egyptian Arabic. It expresses "there is,"
"there are."

    Mohamed fi amriika
    Mohamed is in the States.

    fiih çàràbiyyà gamb ilbeet
    There is a car near the house.

3. We use "ma _____ ʃ" with çand" sentences when
    "çand" means "to have." Previously we said that
    "çand" has more than one meaning ("with," "at,"
    "chez," and "to have"). When we use "çand" as a
    means of expressing "to have" it has a suffix
    pronoun:

    çandi   çandik
    I have   You have

4. We also use "ma _____ ʃ" with the following types
    of sentences:

    ittàràbeezà, çaleeha akl
    The table, on it, there is food.

    ilçàràbiyyà, gowwaaha naas
    The car, in it, there are people.

    We translate these sentences in rather stilted
English. We cannot do otherwise since the very
structure of this type of sentence is particular to
Arabic.

How to Negate with "ma ----- ȼ:

1. If the word surrounded by ma _____ ȼ ends in a
    vowel, the vowel is extended.

    çand<u>i</u>

    ma çand <u>ii</u> ȼ

    çandah<u>a</u>

    maçandah<u>aa</u> ȼ

2. If the word ends in a silent (h), the silent (h)
    will be sounded.

    ilmaktab, <u>fiih</u> mowȧzzȧfiin

    The office, <u>in it</u>, there are employees.

    ilmaktab, mafiihuuȼ mowȧzzȧfiin

TAPE VI/SIDE 1

Negation of the Nominal Sentence

Answer the Following Questions Negatively, Using
"ma ----- ȼ."

fiih mowȧzzȧfiin kitiir?
Are there many employees?
la' mafiiȼ mowȧzzȧfiin kitiir
No, there aren't many employees.

1. Fiih akl kwayyis fil<u>mat</u>çam?
    Is there good food in the <u>restaurant</u>?
    la' mafiiȼ akl kwayyis fi lmȧtçȧm
    No, there isn't good food in the restaurant.

2. Fiih xawagaat kitiir fi màsr?

   Are there many foreigners in Egypt.

   la', mafiiʃ xawagaat kitiir

   No, there aren't many foreigners in Egypt.

3. Fiih mokalmaat kitiir lilmodiir?

   Are there many phone-calls for the manager?

   la' mafiiʃ mokalmaat kitiir lilmodiir

   No, there aren't many phone calls for the manager.

4. Fiih owàd kitiir fiʃʃa"a?

   Are there many rooms in the apartment?

   la', mafiiʃ owàd kitiir fiʃʃa"a

   No, there aren't many rooms in the apartment.

5. ilmàtʃàm, fiih akl kwayyis?

   The restaurant, in it there is good food?

   la', ilmàtʃàm, mafihuuʃ akl kwayyis

   No, the restaurant, in it there isn't good food.

6. Màsr, fiiha xawagaat kitiir?

   Egypt, in it, are there many foreigners?

   la', màsr, mafihaaʃ xawagaat kitiir

   No, Egypt, in it, there aren't many foreigners.

7. ilmodiir, lii(h) mokalmaat?

   The manager, for him, there are phone calls?

   la', ilmodiir malhuuʃ mokalmaat

   No, the manager, for him, there aren't phone calls.

8. iʃʃa"a, fiiha owàd kitiir?

   The apartment, in it there are many rooms?

   la', iʃʃa"a mafihaaʃ owàd kitiir

   No, the apartment, in it there aren't many rooms.

9. ʃandak xamsa we ʃiʃriin sana?

   Are you twenty-five-years old?

la', maçamdiiʃ xamsa we çiʃriin sana

No, I'm not twenty-five-years old.

(Literally: I don't have 25 years.)

10. çandik foluus?

Do you have money?

la', maçandiiʃ foluus

No, I don't have money.

I Was Hungry/I Was Not Hungry

The Nominal Sentence with "Kaan"

The nominal sentence does not contain the verb "to be." However, the verb "to be," i.e., "kaan," does exist in Arabic. It is used to express things other than existence in the present.

"Kaan" has a temporal aspect. It is used with the nominal sentence to express the existence of something in the past. It renders the entire nominal sentence past. For example:

Mohamed mawguud	Mohamed is (present) here.
Mohamed kaan mawguud	Mohamed was (present) here.
John filbeet	John is in the house.
John kaan filbeet	John was in the house.

"Kaan" conjugates like all other verbs, i.e., it changes with different subject pronouns.

The Nominal Sentence with "kaan"

Listen and Repeat

ana kont	I was
inta kont	you were
inti konti	you were
howwa kaan	he was
hiyya kaanit	she was
ihna konna	we were
intu kontu	you were

Put the Following Sentences in the Past Tense Using the Correct Form of "kaan"

1. ana taçbaan   I am tired.
   ana kont taçbaan   I was tired.

2. inta zaçlaan?   Are you upset?
   inta kont zaçlaan?   Were you upset?

3. inti šåtrå   You are clever.
   inti konti šåtrå   You were clever.

4. howwa çaawiz šaay   He wants tea.
   howwa kaan çaawiz šaay   He wanted tea.

5. hiyya çawza ahwa   She wants coffee.
   hiyya kaanit çawza ahwa   She wanted coffee.

6. ihna mawgudiin filbeet   We are (present) at home.
   ihna konna mawgudiin filbeet   We were at home.

7. intu gaçaniin?   Are you hungry?
   intu kontu gaçaniin?   Were you hungry?

8. homma çandohom çåråbiyyå   They have a car.
   homma kaan çandohom çåråbiyyå   They had a car.

Put the Following Sentences in the Past Tense Using the
Correct Form of "kaan" According to the Subject
Pronoun:

1. ilmodiir fi beetu(h)   ilomodiir kaan fi
                                 beetu(h)

2. Mohamed çandi   Mohamed kaan çandi

3. ana fillokåndå   ana kont fi llokåndå

4. hiyya taçbaana   hiyya kaanit taçbaana

5. ihna zaçlaniin   ihna konna zaçlaniin

6. ana fi måsr   ana kont fi måsr

7. homma fi amriika   homma kaanu fĭ amriika

8. Nadia çawza måyyå   Nadia kaanit çawza måyyå

9. ihna çawziin ǧa"a   ihna konna çawziin ǧa"a

10. ilfoluus çala lmaktab   ilfoluus kannit çala
                                 lmaktab

NOTE:

With certain types of nominal sentences "kaan" will not
conjugate. It will remain "kaan" throughout. Here are
examples:

1. wåråäyå ǧoġl

    I have work. (Literally: I have work behind me.)

    kaan wåråäyå ǧoġl

2. wåråäna ǧoġl

    kaan wåråäna ǧoġl

3. çandaha foluus

    kaan çandaha foluus

4. çandu(h) foluus

    kaan çandu(h) foluus

"Kaan" does not change with these sentences even
when the subject pronoun changes.

The Nominal Sentence with "kaan"

Render the Following Sentences Past by Using "kaan"

1. ilmodiir, wåråå(h) ⁄oġl
   kaan wåråå(h) ⁄oġl
2. i⁄⁄irka, fiiha foluus
   kaan fiiha foluus
3. ittåråbeezå gambaha korsi
   kaan gambaha korsi
4. ikkorsi çaleeh alam   (pen)
   kaan çaleeh alam
5. fiih akl filbeet?
   kaan fiih akl filbeet?
6. maçaana foluus
   kaan maçaana foluus
7. fiih talat çåråbiyyååt fi⁄⁄aariç
   kaan fiih talat çåråbiyyååt if⁄⁄aariç
8. ilbalad fiiha årbåç lokåndååt   (country)
   ilbalad kaan fiiha årbåç lokåndååt
9. çalayya ⁄eek
   kaan çalayya ⁄eek
10. çaleena deen   (debt)
    kaan çaleena deen

Negation of the Nominal Sentence with "kaan"

Review of Negation of the Nominal Sentence:

1. Mohamed mawguud

   la', Mohamed mi$ mawguud

2. fiih akl filbeet

   la', mafii$ akl filbeet

3. ilmodiir çandu(h) $oġl

   la', ilmodiir maçanduu$ $oġl

Negation of the Nominal Sentence with "kaan"

1. We negate the nominal sentence with "kaan" by using "ma _____ $."

2. "Ma _____ $" surrounds the verb "kaan" in the sentence.

3. In using "ma _____ $" with "kaan" we will apply our basic categories of words ending with:

   a. C   (consonant)
   b. CC   (two consonants)
   c. V   (vowel)

ana kont	CC
inta kont	CC
inti konti	V
howwa kaan	C
hiyya kaanit	C
ihna konna	V

intu kont<u>u</u>   V

homma kaan<u>u</u>   V

You already know that:

1. If a word ends with a C we can simply add another
    C:

    howwa kaa<u>n</u>   C

    howwa ma kan̸   CC

2. If a word ends in CC we simply <u>cannot</u> add a third
    C. It is not allowed in Egyptian Arabic. We must
    use a <u>helping vowel</u>.

    ana ko<u>nt</u>   CC

    ana mako<u>nti</u≯   CC i C

3. If the word ends in a vowel we simply add another
    vowel, then we suffix "̸":

    ihna konna
    .

    ihna mako<u>nnaa</u≯   VV̸
    .

TAPE VI/SIDE 2

Negation of the Nominal Sentence with "kaan"

Negation of "kaan"

ana kont	ana makonti̸
inta kont	inta makonti̸
inti konti	inti makontii̸
howwa kaan	howwa makan̸
hiyya kannit	hiyya makanit̸
ihna konna	ihna makonnaa̸
.	.

```
intu kontu          intu makontuuʂ

homma kaanu         homma makanuuʂ
```

Respond to the Following Questions Negatively Using "kaan"

1. ilmodiir kaan wårååh ʂoġl?

2. Mohamed kaan çandak?

3. inta kont fi llikåndå?

4. hiyya kaanit taçbaana?

5. homma kaanu zaçlaniin?

6. intu kontu fi måsr?

7. Nadia kaanit çawza ʂa"a?

8. inti konti çawza ʂa"a?

9. intu kontu çawziin <u>haaga</u>?   (something)

10. ilfoluus kaanit çala lmaktab?

11. ittåråbeezå kaan gambaha korsi?

12. ikkorsi kaan çaleeh alam?

13. kaan fiih ʂa"a <u>fådyå</u>?   (empty)

14. kaan fiih akl fi ttallaaga?   (refrigerator)

15. kaan fiih <u>çåsiir</u> fi kkobbaaya?   (juice)

16. ilbalad kaan fiiha årbåç lokåndååt?

17. kaan çandoku føluus?

18. kaan maçaaha çåråbiyyå?

TAPE VI/SIDE 2

Review Drills

Translate into Arabic

(On tape--no transcriptions)

Doing Things

The Verb

Before we actually treat the verb, let us explain the basic logic behind Arabic as a language.

Arabic has a <u>root</u> system. A <u>root</u> is the <u>naked form</u> from which a given word derives. To put it differently, we can say that, given a basic root in Arabic, we can form different words that have different functions. We can add a prefix, a suffix or both to the base <u>root</u>. Sometimes we lengthen a vowel in the root, or double one of its consonants. The important point is that we are able to create many words that derive from the same root.

Every <u>root</u> has a <u>basic meaning</u>. Any word that derives from a given root will retain that basic meaning, in one form or the other. Let us take some examples:

Root	kataba	to write
	katab	to write
	kattib	to cause to write
	kaatib	one who writes
	kitaab	a book
	maktab	a desk (object on which one writes)
	maktaba	library (place where written books are kept)
	maktuub	that which is written
	kit aaba	the act of writing
	inkatab	to be written
	kottaab	a place where one learns writing (school)

1. All these words derive from the basic root (kataba).

2. It is important to know the root of a word to find out its meaning in a dictionary. Arabic dictionaries enter words under the root from which they are derived. The above words would be entries under "kataba."

3. Notice that all derived words retain not only the meaning but also the basic skeleton of that root. They all have the three consonants that form the basic root (k - t - b).

4. Some of these words are verbs, others are nouns ... etc. You will be able to make up your own derived words once you know the pattern and forms that govern verbs and nouns respectively.

5. Every verb derives from a basic root. We have twelve derived forms of the verb. For example:

Original Roots	Derived Forms of Verb
daras	darris (form II)
ibil	aabil (form III)
çamal	itçamal (form VII)
dåråb	dåårib (form III)

Notice that in one case we doubled a consonant of the root, in another we added a prefix, and in a third we lengthened the vowel.

6. Each derived form of the verb connotes a basic meaning. Every derived form has its own characteristics. Let us take an example. The second derived form (form II) is characterized by the doubling of the middle consonant of the root:

da<u>r</u>as	da<u>rr</u>is
ka<u>t</u>ab	ka<u>tt</u>ib
da<u>x</u>al	da<u>xx</u>al
wå<u>s</u>ål	wå<u>ss</u>ål

The <u>second form</u> is primarily a <u>causative</u> form,
i.e., its basic meaning is "to cause someone to do
something." Let us return to the above examples
once more:

Verb Form I	Meaning	Verb Form II	Meaning
katab	to write	kattib	to cause to write
daxal	to enter	daxxal	to cause to enter
wàsàl	to arrive	wassal	to cause to arrive (give someone a lift)

If you keep the points above in mind, you will be
able to trace words to a root, or even another word that
you may know. You will be able to guess the meaning of
words you have never seen before.

Supposing I know the word <u>mafhuum</u> (understood) and
I hear someone say "ana <u>faahim</u>." With a little bit of
guess-work and some familiarity with the root system we
can conclude that the word "<u>faahim</u>" has something to do
with understanding.

This is a later stage in language learning.
However it's good to be conscious of the <u>Method of
reasoning</u> now.

<u>Verb</u> means <u>Action</u>. <u>Actions</u> are either <u>complete</u>
(<u>perfect</u>) or <u>incomplete</u> (imperfect). They are <u>complete</u>
(perfect) in the sense that they are <u>finished</u>, <u>done</u>,
<u>accomplished</u> i.e. <u>past</u>. They are <u>incomplete</u> (imperfect)
in the sense that they are <u>not finished</u>. The <u>imperfect</u>
verb, therefore, stands for an <u>incomplete action</u>. An
incomplete action can be happening right <u>now</u> (present),
it can be something that will happen in the <u>future</u>, or
it can even be an <u>order</u> that has not yet been carried
out, or completed. Let us think of verbs in Arabic
along these lines:

perfect (complete)	imperfect (incomplete)

1. <u>A given verb</u> looks different in the perfect from
    what it is like in the imperfect.

perfect	imperfect
<u>kat</u>ab	yi<u>kt</u>ib
<u>til</u>iç	yi<u>tla</u>ç

2. Notice that even though the same verb looks a bit
    different in each case (perfect/imperfect) it still
    retains the skeletal root.

3. "katab" is perfect. It means "wrote." It is <u>past</u>.
    The action of writing has been completed.

    "yiktib" is an imperfect because it is <u>incomplete</u>
    as an action. By adding certain prefixes to
    "yiktib" we can obtain variations on incomplete
    actions (present, future, commands).

4. You will always need to learn both the perfect and
    the imperfect together. Just like plural patterns
    of nouns, the imperfect verb is unpredictable. "To
    go" means "ráàḥ" in Arabic. The imperfect of ráàḥ"
    is "yir<u>uu</u>ḥ." The vowel is "<u>uu</u>" and not "<u>aa</u>" as in
    the perfect.

    We will give you a list of more than 150 verbs in
    both perfect and imperfect forms. Memorize the
    <u>imperfect</u> of ten verbs each day.

    This side of the tape contains a list of verbs. We
    want you to listen and repeat. We will give you
    things in the following order:

    a. Verb – <u>perfect</u>
    b. Meaning in English
    c. Same verb in the <u>imperfect</u>.

    The 150 verbs on this list are just a beginning.
Add to your verb list from any sources you can find
(people on the street – school, etc.). Follow our
system when you make additions. All verbs are given in
the third person masculine singular, i.e., "he." This
is standard in Arabic.

A List of Verbs in the Perfect Tense

Listen and Repeat

Form I (strong = 3 consonants)   Group (a - a) (CVCVC)

Perfect	Meaning	Imperfect
s̸árȧh (li)	to explain (to)	yis̸rȧh
sa'al	to ask	yis'al
wȧsȧl (min)	to arrive (from)	yiwsȧl
dafaç	to pay	yidfaç
daras	to study	yidris
ça,a;	to do	yiçmil
katab (li)	to write (to)	yiktib
çagab	to admire/like	yiçgtib
tȧlȧb	to order/request	yitlob
açad	to sit/remain	yi'çod
fatah	to open	yiftah
afal	to close/shut	yi'fil
daxal	to enter	yidxol
xȧrȧg	to go out/exit	yixrog

Form I (strong = 3 consonants)   Group (i - i)   (CVCVC)

Perfect	Meaning	Imperfect
fihim	to understand	yifham
çirif (inn)	to know (that)	yiçrȧf
s̸irib	to drink	yis̸rȧb
tiliç	to go up	yitlȧç
tiçib (min)	to be tired (of)	yitçab
çitis̸	to be thirsty	yiçtȧs̸
fitit	to breakfast	yiftȧr

111

Perfect	Meaning	Imperfect
idir	to be able/capable	yi'dȧr
wi'if	to stand up	yu'af
xiḷis	to be finished/ completed	yixlȧs
ziçil	to be upset/angry	yizçal
nizil	to go down	yinzil
libis	to get dressed	yilbis
rikib	to ride	yirkab

Form I (Weak = ending in a vowel) Group (a - a) (CVCV)

Perfect	Meaning	Imperfect
ȧrȧ	to read	yi'rȧ
mȧdȧ	to sign	yimḍi
la'a	to find	yilaa'i
kawa	to press/iron	yikwi
ḥaka	to tell (a story)	yihki
ba'a	to stay/remain/ become	yib'a
ǵaka	to complain	yiǵki
nafa	to negate	yinfi

Form I (Weak = ending in a vowel) Group (i - i) (CVCV)

Perfect	Meaning	Imperfect
miǵi	to walk/to leave	yimǵi
nisi	to forget	yinsa
sihi	to wake up	yisha

Form I (Hollow = 2 consonants/long vowel)   (CVVC)

Perfect	Meaning	Imperfect
kaan	to be	yikuun
aal (inn)	to say (that)	yi'uul
şaaf (inn)	to see/to believe (that)	yişuuf
çaaz	to want/need	yiçuuz
ráàh	to go	yiruuh
faat (çala)	to pass (by)	yifuut
gaaç	to be hungry	yiguuç
saa'	to drive	yisuu'
aam	to stand up	yi'uum
şaal	to carry	yişiil
gaab	to bring	yigiib
baaç	to sell	yibiiç
naam	to sleep	yinaam
çaaş	to live	yiçiiş

Form I (Doubled = 3 cons./ends in double consonant) (CVCC)

Perfect	Meaning	Imperfect
rádd (çala)	to answer	yirodd
habb	to love/like	yihibb
tamm	to be completed	yitimm
hazz	to shake	yihizz
báss (çala)	to look (on)	yiboss
xaşş	to enter	yixoşş
şakk	to doubt	yişokk
zann	to nag	yizinn

Form II (Causative/Intensive/Declarative)   (CVCCVC)

Perfect	Meaning	Imperfect
fahhim	to explain (cause to understand)	yifahhim
darris	to teach (cause to study)	yidarris
kallim	to speak to	yikallim
nazzil	to bring down (cause to come down)	yinazzil
çallim	to teach	yiçallim
akkil	to feed (cause to eat)	yi'akkil
sallif	to lend	yisallif
sahhil	to make easy; facilitate	yisahhil
ŝàrràb	to cause to drink	yiŝàrràb
fàttàr	to cause to breakfast	yifàttàr
ŝaġġal	to cause to work; employ	yiŝaġġal
wàssàl	to cause to arrive	yiwàssàl
daffaç	to cause to pay	yidaffaç
tàllàç	to cause to group; to take up	yitàllàç
fàkkàr	to think	yifàkkàr
dàwwàr (çala)	to look for	yidàwwàr
sallim (çala)	to greet; say hello	yisallim
nàddàf	to clean	yinàddàf
sàllàh	to repair	yisàllàh
wàddàh	to make clear	yiwàddàh
ràwwàh	to go <u>home</u>	yiràwwàh

Perfect	Meaning	Imperfect
gȧrrȧb	to try	yigȧrrȧb
xȧllȧs	to finish; complete	yixȧllȧs
zaçҫal	to cause to be upset	yizaçҫal
çaʂʂa	to take to dinner; cause to dine	yiçaʂʂi
ġadda	to take to lunch; cause to lunch	yiġaddi
idda	to give	yiddi
warra	to show	yiwarri
wadda	to deliver to; take to someone	yiwaddi
sȧhhȧ	to cause to wake up	yisȧhhi
nassa	to cause to forget	yinassi
fȧddȧl	to prefer	yifȧddȧl
xalla	to keep	yixalli

Form III   (CVVCVC)

Perfect	Meaning	Imperfect
fȧȧsil	to bargain	yifȧȧsil
saaçid	to help	yisaaçid
tȧȧlib	to demand	yitȧȧlib
saafir	to depart (on a trip)	yisaafir
hȧȧwil	to try	yihȧȧwil
aabil	to meet	yi'aabil
gaawib	to answer	yigaawib
naa'iʂ	to discuss	yinaa'iʂ
haasib	to make accounts with	yihaasib

115

Perfect	Meaning	Imperfect
waafi'	to agree; to give one's consent	yiwaafi'
çaamil	to treat	yiçaamil

Form V (it + CVCCVC) Note the relationship between
Forms II and V.

Perfect	Meaning	Imperfect
itkallim (maça)	to speak with	yitkallim
itçallim	to learn	yitçallim
itçàrràf (çala)	to make someone's acquaintance	yitçàrràf
itġadda	to have lunch	yitġadda
itça$$a	to have dinner	yitça$$a
itsàrràf	to manage on one's own	yitsàrràf
itfàddàl	a polite form of offering	yitfàddàl

Form VI (it + CVVCVC) Note the relationship between
Form III and VI.

Perfect	Meaning	Imperfect
itnaa'i$ (maça)	to discuss (with)	yitnaa'i$
itfaahim (maça)	to reach an understanding with	yitfaahim
it'aabil	to meet with	yit'aabil
ithaasib (maça)	to settle accounts (with)	yithaasib
itxaani' (maça)	to argue (with)	yitxaani'
itçaamil (maça)	to deal (with)	yitçaamil

116

Form VII   (it + CVCVC)   Note the relationship between
   Form I and VII.

Perfect	Meaning	Imperfect
itçamal	was done	yitçimil
itbaaç	was sold	yitbaaç
itfaham	was understood	yitfihim
itmàḍà	was signed	yitmidi
itkatab	was written	yitkitib
itçàràf	was known	yitçirif
it'afal	was closed	yit'ifil

Form VIII

Perfect	Meaning	Imperfect
iȿtara	to buy	yiȿtiri
ihtàràm	to respect	yihtirim
iftàkàr	to remember	yiftikir
istalaf	to borrow	yistilif
igtamaç (bi)	to meet (with)	yigtimiç
iȿtàràk	to participate	yiȿtirik
ibtada	to begin; commence	yibtidi
intaha	to end; terminate	yintihi
iȿtaġal	to work	yiȿtaġal

Form X

Perfect	Meaning	Imperfect
ista'bil	to receive someone	yista'bil
istaçmil	to use	yistaçmil
istanna	to wait	yistanna
istahamma	to wash oneself	yistahamma

REMARKS:

1. If you remember the <u>sound</u> of these <u>groups</u> of verbs
    the way we presented them, you will be able to
    conjugate verbs that <u>sound</u> similar to ones you
    know. For example "<u>daras</u>" is one verb you know.
    If you know how to conjugate it, then you will know
    how to conjugate <u>katab</u> even if you are seeing it
    for the first time.

Doing Things
(continuation)

The Perfect and the Imperfect

The list of verbs in the previous section divided
the verbs into groups. Each group of verbs has its own
way of conjugation. This means that if you know one
verb from one group (e.g.: Form I/Group a - a d<u>a</u>r<u>a</u>s)
you will be able to conjugate any other verb that
belongs to that same group (e.g.: k<u>at</u>ab - x<u>à</u>r<u>à</u>b).

To familiarize you with the verb groups we will
give you one example of each. Each verb will appear in
both: <u>perfect</u> and <u>imperfect</u> forms. The following will
be our categories:

1. Form I   Group a - a.   (d<u>a</u>r<u>a</u>s)

2. Form I   Group i - i.   (t<u>il</u>iç)

3. Form III   (haawil)

4. All verbs ending in C.
    (regardless of derived form).

5. All verbs ending in CC.
    (regardless of derived form).

6. All verbs ending in V.
    (regardless of form).

A List of Verbs in the Perfect and Imperfect Tenses

Listen and repeat.

Form I/Group (a - a)

daxal   to enter

perfect (daxal)/imperfect (yidxol)

PERFECT			IMPERFECT		
pronoun	verb	suffix	pronoun	verb	suffix
ana	daxal	t	ana	adxol	
inta	daxal	t	inta	todxol	
inti	daxal	ti	inti	todxol	i
howwa	daxal	--	howwa	yodxol	
hiyya	daxal	it	hiyya	todxol	
ihna	daxal	na	ihna	nodxol	
intu	daxal	tu	intu	todxol	u
homma	daxal	u	homma	yodxol	u

xàràg   to go out

perfect (xàràg)/imperfect (yixrog)

PERFECT			IMPERFECT		
pronoun	verb	suffix	pronoun	verb	suffix
ana	xàràg	t	ana	àxrog	
inta	xàràg	t	inta	toxrog	
inti	xàràg	ti	inti	toxrog	i
howwa	xàràg	--	howwa	yoxrog	
hiyya	xàràg	it	hiyya	toxrog	
ihna	xàràg	na	ihna	noxrog	
intu	xàràg	tu	intu	toxrog	u
homma	xàràg	u	homma	yoxrog	u

REMARKS:

1.   The vowel of the imperfect is unpredictable.
      Not all verbs that belong to the previous
      group look like (yidxol, yixrog) in the
      imperfect. Some look like this: yidfaç,
      yidris. You must therefore learn the
      imperfect.

2.   In our following sections we will show you how we
      add prefixes to the naked imperfect in order to
      form different tenses: present, future,
      commands...etc.

3.   It is important that you know your imperfect since
      it is the basis for forming so many other tenses.

TAPE VII/SIDE 2

Listen and Repeat

Form I/Group (i - i)

nizil   to go down

perfect (nizil)/imperfect (yinzil)

PERFECT			IMPERFECT		
pronoun	verb	suffix	pronoun	verb	suffix
ana	nizil	t	ana	anzil	
inta	nizil	t	inta	tinzil	
inti	nizil	ti	inti	tinzil i	
howwa	nizil	--	howwa	yinzil	
hiyya	nizl	it	hiyya	tinzil	
ihna	nizil	na	ihna	ninzil	
intu	nizil	tu	intu	tinzil u	
homma	nizl	u	homma	yinzil u	

120

Listen and Repeat

Form I (hollow CVVC)

(raah – kaan – ṣaaf – naam)

<u>naam</u>   <u>to sleep</u>

perfect (naam)/imperfect (yinaam)

	PERFECT			IMPERFECT	
<u>pronoun</u>	<u>verb</u>	<u>suffix</u>	<u>pronoun</u>	<u>verb</u>	<u>suffix</u>
ana	nim	t	ana	anaam	
inta	nim	t	inta	tinaam	
inti	nim	ti	inti	tinaam	i
howwa	naam	--	howwa	yinaam	
hiyya	naam	it	hiyya	tinaam	
ihna	nim	na	ihna	ninaam	
intu	nim	tu	intu	tinaam	u
homma	naam	u	homma	yinaam	u

Form I

(xad – kal)

(to take – to eat)

<u>xad</u>   <u>to take</u>

perfect (xad)/imperfect (yaaxud)

	PERFECT			IMPERFECT	
<u>pronoun</u>	<u>verb</u>	<u>suffix</u>	<u>pronoun</u>	<u>verb</u>	<u>suffix</u>
ana	xad	t	ana	aaxod	
inta	xad	t	inta	taaxod	
inti	xad	ti	inti	taxd	i
howwa	xad	--	howwa	yaaxod	
hiyya	xad	it	hiyya	taaxod	

pronoun	verb	suffix	pronoun	verb	suffix
iḥna	xad	na	iḥna	naaxod	
intu	xad	tu	intu	taxd	u
homma	xad	u	homma	yaxd	u

Form III

saaçid   to help

perfect (saaçid)/imperfect (yisaaçid)

	PERFECT			IMPERFECT	
pronoun	verb	suffix	pronoun	verb	suffix
ana	saçid	t	ana	asaaçid	
inta	saçid	t	inta	tisaaçid	
inti	saçid	ti	inti	tisaçd	i
howwa	saaçid	--	howwa	yisaaçid	
hiyya	saçd	it	hiyya	tisaaçid	
iḥna	saçid	na	iḥna	nissaçid	
intu	saçid	tu	intu	tisaçd	u
homma	saçd	u	homma	yisaçd	u

Verbs ending in C

(itçallim - itnaa'iş - itçamal)

itçallim   to learn

perfect (itçallim)/imperfect (yitçallim)

	PERFECT			IMPERFECT	
pronoun	verb	suffix	pronoun	verb	suffix
ana	ítçallim	t	ana	atçallim	
inta	ítçallim	t	inta	titçallim	
inti	itçallim	ti	inti	titçallim	i
howwa	itçallim	--	howwa	yitçallim	

pronoun	verb	suffix	pronoun	verb	suffix
hiyya	itçallim	it	hiyya	titçallim	
ihna	itçallim	na	ihna	nitçallim	
intu	itçallim	tu	intu	titçallim	u
homma	itçallim	u	homma	yitçallim	u

Verbs ending in CC

(rådd – habb – itlamm – ihtamm)

habb   to like/love

perfect (habb)/imperfect (yihibb)

	PERFECT			IMPERFECT	
pronoun	verb	suffix	pronoun	verb	suffix
ana	habb	eet	ana	ahibb	
inta	habb	eet	inta	tihibb	
inti	habb	eeti	inti	tihibb	i
howwa	habb	----	howwa	yihibb	
hiyya	habb	it	hiyya	tihibb	
ihna	habb	eena	ihna	nihibb	
intu	habb	eetu	intu	tihibb	u
homma	habb	u	homma	yihibb	u

Verbs ending in V

(miśi – nisi – kawa – la'a)

nisi   to forget

perfect (nisi)/imperfect (yinsa)

	PERFECT			IMPERFECT	
pronoun	verb	suffix	pronoun	verb	suffix
ana	nisi	it	ana	ansa	
inta	nisi	it	inta	tinsa	

pronoun	verb	suffix	pronoun	verb	suffix
inti	nisi	iti	inti	tins	i
howwa	nisi	---	howwa	yinsa	
hiyya	nisy	it	hiyya	tinsa	
ihna	nisi	ina	ihna	ninsa	
intu	nisi	itu	intu	tins	u
homma	nisy	u	homma	yins	u

Note: With verbs ending in <u>V</u> that final vowel is
doubled, i.e. if the vowel is <u>a</u>, it becomes aa.

Irregular Verb

<u>geh</u>   to come

perfect (geh)/imperfect (yiigi)

PERFECT   IMPERFECT

pronoun	verb	suffix	pronoun	verb	suffix
ana	gee	t	ana	aagi	
inta	gee	t	inta	tiigi	
inti	gee	ti	inti	tiigi	
howwa	geh/gah	--	howwa	yiigi	
hiyya	gat	--	hiyya	tiigi	
ihna	gee	na	ihna	niigi	
intu	geet	u	intu	tiig	u
homma	gom	-	homma	yiig	u

What Happened Yesterday

The Perfect Tense of the Verb

The verbal sentence contains a verb. The basic characteristics of the verbal sentence are:

1. The verb almost always follows the subject.

    ana daxalt il'oodȧ

    I entered the room.

2. The verb agrees with the subject by the addition of a suffix.

    inta daxalt
    inti daxalti
    intu daxaltu

3. The subject need not always appear in the sentence. It will be understood from the suffix on the verb.

    ihna daxalna

    We entered.

    Daxalna

    We entered.

The verb in the perfect tense is really the English past tense. All actions expressed through the perfect tense are complete actions.

TAPE VIII/ SIDE 1

The Perfect Tense of the Verb

Conjugate the following:

1. howwa wȧsȧl imbaarih
   He arrived yesterday.

ana	wȧsȧlt imbaarih
inta	wȧsȧlt imbaarih
inti	wȧsȧlti mbaarih
hiyya	wȧsȧlit imbarrih
ihna	wȧsȧlnȧ mbaarih
intu	wȧsȧltu mbaarih
homma	wȧsȧlu mbaarih

2. howwa dafaç ilhisaab
   He paid the cheque.

ana	dafaçt ilhisaab
inta	dafaçt ilhisaab
inti	dafaçti ihisaab
hiyya	dafaçit ilhisaab
ihna	dafaçna lhisaab
intu	dafaçtu lhisaab
homma	dafaçu lhisaab

3. howwa çamal ʃoġlu
   He did his work.

ana	çamalt ʃoġli
ihna	çamalna ʃoġlina
inti	çamalti ʃoġlik
homma	çamalu ʃoġlohom
intu	çamaltu ʃoġloku
hiyya	çamalit ʃoġlaha
inta	çamalt ʃoġlak

4. howwa fiṭir <u>badri</u>

He (breakfasted) <u>early</u>.

ana	fiṭirt badri
inta	fiṭirt badri
inti	fiṭirti badri

howwa fiṭir <u>waxri</u>

He (breakfasted) <u>late</u>.

hiyya	fiṭrit waxri
ihna	fiṭirna waxri
intu	fiṭirtu waxri
homma	fiṭru waxri

5. howwa <u>nizil ilbalad</u>

He <u>went down town</u>. (expression)

ana	nizilt ilbalad
inta	nizilt ilbalad
inti	nizilti ilbalad
hiyya	nizlit ilbalad

howwa <u>nizil taḥt</u>

He <u>went downstairs</u>.

ihna	nizilna taḥt
intu	niziltu taḥt
homma	nizlu taḥt

6. howwa nisi nimrit ittilifoon

He forgot the phone number.

ana	nisiit nimrit ittilifoon
inta	nisiit nimrit ittilifoon
inti	nisiiti nimrit ittilifoon
hiyya	nisyit nimrit ittilifoon
ihna	nisiina nimrit ittilifoon
intu	nisiitu nimrit ittilifoon

```
       homma          nisyu nimrit ittilifoon
7.     howwa la'a ǵa"a
       He found an apartment.
       ana            la'eet ǵa"a
       inta           la'eet ǵa"a
       inti           la'eeti ǵa"a
       hiyya          la'et ǵa"a
       howwa la'a lҫinwaan
       He found the address.
       ihna           la'eena lҫinwaan
       intu           la'eetu lҫinwaan
       homma          la'u lҫinwaan
8.     howwa rååh illokåndå lwahdu
       He went to the hotel alone.  (by himself)
       ana            roht illokåndå lwahdi
       inta           roht illokåndå lwahdak
       inti           rohti llokåndå lwahdik
       hiyya          rååhit illokåndå lwahdaha
       ihna           rohna llokåndå lwahdina
       intu           rohtu llokåndå lwahdoku
       homma          rååhu llokåndå lwahdohom
9.     howwa baaҫ ilmahall
       He sold the shop.
       ana            biҫt ilmahall
       inta           biҫt ilmahall
       inti           biҫti lmahall
       hiyya          baaҫit ilmahall
       howwa baaҫ nafsu  (nafs - the self)
       He sold himself.  (expression) (negative
                                   connotation)
```

ihna	biçna nafsina
intu	biçtu nafsoku
homma	baaçu nafsohom

10. howwa <u>hått</u> ilfoluus filbank

He <u>put</u> the money in the bank.

ana	håtteet ilfoluus filbank
inta	håtteet ilfoluus filbank
inti	håtteeti ilfoluus filbank
hiyya	håttet ilfoluus filbank

howwa hått <u>ilhagaat gowwa</u>

He put <u>the things inside.</u>

ihna	håtteena lhagaat gowwa
intu	håtteetu lhagaat gowwa
homma	håttu lhagaat gowwa

11. howwa habb ilbalad

He liked the country.

hiyya	habbit ilbalad
ana	habbeet ilbalad
inta	habbeet ilbalad

howwa habb <u>ilmasriyyiin</u>

He liked <u>the Egyptians.</u>

ihna	habbeena ilmåsriyiin
intu	habbeetu ilmåsriyiin
homma	habbu ilmåsriyiin

12. howwa fåkkår <u>filmåwduuç</u>

He thought about <u>the subject</u>.

ihna	fåkkårnå filmåwduuç
hiyya	fåkkårit filmåwduuç
inta	fåkkårt filmåwduuç

homma	fȧkkȧru filmȧwduuҫ
inti	fȧkkȧrti filmȧwduuҫ
intu	fȧkkȧrtu filmȧwduuҫ
ana	fȧkkȧrt filmȧwduuҫ

13. howwa idda Nadia <u>hidiyya</u>

He gave Nadia <u>a present</u>.

ihna	iddeena Nadia hidiyya
intu	iddeetu Nadia hidiyya
ana	iddeet Nadia hiddiyya
hiyya	iddit Nadia hidiiyya

howwa idda lmowȧzzȧfiin <u>mokaf'a</u>.

He gave the employees a <u>bonus</u>. (reward)

homma	iddu lmowȧzzȧfiin mokaf'a
inta	iddeet ilmowȧzzȧfiin mokaf'a

14. howwa saafir amriika

He traveled to the USA.

ana	safirt amriika
inta	safirt amriika
inti	safirti amriika
hiyya	safrit amriika

howwa saafir ilyabaan

He traveled to Japan.

ihna	safirna lyabaan
intu	safirtu lyabaan
homma	safru lyabaan

15. howwa kal <u>samak</u>

He ate <u>fish</u>.

ana	kalt samak
inta	kalt samak
inti	kalti samak

hiyya	kalit samak
ihna	kalna samak
intu	kaltu samak
homma	kalu samak

What Did Not Happen Yesterday

Negation of the Perfect

1. We negate the <u>perfect</u> by using "ma _____ ȼ."

2. "ma _____ ȼ" surrounds the verb in the sentence.

    ana daxalt   I entered.

    ana <u>ma</u>daxalti<u>ȼ</u>   I didn't enter.

3. In suffixing " _____ ȼ" on to the verb, we will still go by our rule for words that end in C / CC / V.

    a. If the verb in the sentence ends in a C we just add "ȼ."

       hiyya daxali<u>t</u>   C

       She entered.

       hiyya ma daxalitȼ   Cȼ

    b. If the verb in the sentence ends in CC we <u>must</u> add a helping vowel before suffixing "ȼ" to avoid the sequence CCC.

       ana daxa<u>lt</u>   CC

       I entered.

       ana madaxalti<u>ȼ</u>   CCiȼ

c. If the verb in the sentence ends in a $\underline{V}$ we must lengthen the vowel to $\underline{VV}$ and then add "$\not{s}$."

howwa kaw<u>a</u> lbántáloon   V

He ironed the trousers.

howwa makaw<u>aa</u>$\not{s}$ ......   VV$\not{s}$

He didn't iron the trousers.

We will return to the drills on Tape VIII/Side 1 and negate the statements made there. You may refer to the transcriptions of Tape VIII/Side 1 in doing the following drills.

TAPE VIII/SIDE 2

Negation of the Perfect

Negate the following sentences by using "ma ---- $\not{s}$":

Please use transcriptions of Tape VIII/Side 1 for the drills on this side of the tape.

Expressing Desire, Probability, Possibility and Obligation

The Imperfect

The verb in the imperfect is a <u>naked form</u>. It is a means of expressing an <u>incomplete action</u>. The imperfect provides the base for forming other tenses. Once we add certain prefixes to the naked imperfect we obtain the present tense and the future. What good is the imperfect as a naked form?

If we consider that incomplete actions can be many things other than present and future, then the naked imperfect will make sense. Here are the different usages of the imperfect:

1. It is used in a sequence of two verbs as a helping verb.

    roht <u>aakol</u>

    I went <u>to eat</u>.

    omt <u>ağråb</u>

    I got up <u>to drink</u>.

In a sequence of two verbs, the second verb will always be imperfect. In this case the imperfect funtions like the English infinitive: to eat, to drink, to sleep.

2. The imperfect is the means by which we express <u>desire</u>, <u>want</u> or <u>need</u>:

    çaawiz ağråb

    I want to drink.

    çawziin niğråb

    We want to drink.

Here are words which will <u>always be followed by the</u>
<u>imperfect</u>:

    a. çaawiz

        çawza   want

        çawziin

    b. nifsi

        nifsak   to be dying to do something

        nifsik

        nifsu(h)

        nifsaha

        nifsina

          etc. ...

    c. yareet   if only you would ....

3.   The imperfect is the means by which we express
<u>obligation</u>, <u>must</u>, <u>urgency</u>.

<u>Laazim tiɟràb</u>

You <u>must</u> drink.

<u>Laazim tiɟràbu</u>

You must drink.

Laazim is <u>constant</u> with all pronouns.

Here are some words which express obligation. Like
<u>laazim</u>, they are constant.

    màfruud   It is a must that ...

    dàruuri   It is important that ...

4.   The imperfect is the means of expressing
<u>possibility</u>, <u>questioning possibility</u> or <u>asserting</u>
<u>possibility</u>:

<u>momkin</u> aɟràb?

<u>May</u> I drink?

aywa, momkin ti/ràb

Yes, you **may** drink.

5. The imperfect is used to <u>question desire of others,</u> and to <u>question capability</u>. In this case we have a <u>sequence of two imperfect verbs:</u>

tihibb ti/ràb?

Would you like to drink?

tihibbu ti/ràbu?

Would you like to drink?

Here are some verbs that fit in this category:

tiçraf	Do you know how to ...
ti'dàr	Can you ...
tismah	Would you permit that ...
tihibb	Would you like to ...

NOTE: there has to be a sequence of <u>two</u> imperfects.

6. The imperfect is used to express <u>probability</u>.

<u>gaayiz</u> àxrog

I might go out.

<u>gaayiz</u> noxrog

We might go out.

<u>Gaayiz</u> is constant with all pronouns.

Here are other words that express <u>probability</u>:

yimkin	might
ihtimaal	there is a probability that

"Yimkin," and "ihtimaal," like "gaayiz," are constant.

The Imperfect Tense of the Verb

Please listen and repeat

1. howwa <u>nizil yiʃtiri xodáàr</u>
    He went down to buy <u>vegetables.</u>

ana	nizilt aʃtiri ...
inta	nizilt tiʃtiri ... ?
inti	nizilti tiʃtiri ... ? iʃtara (yiʃtiri)
hiyya	nizlit tiʃtiri ... to buy
ihna	nizilna niʃtiri ...
intu	niziltu tiʃtiru ... ?
homma	nizlu yiʃtiru ...

2. howwa çaawiz yiʃràb <u>ʃaay</u>
    He wants to drink <u>tea.</u>

ana	çawza aʃràb ʃaay
inta	çaawiz tiʃràb ʃaay?
inti	çawza tiʃràbi ʃaay? ʃirib (yiʃràb)
hiyya	çawza tiʃràb ʃaay to drink
howwa	çaawiz yiʃràb ahwa
ihna	çawziin niʃràb ahwa
intu	çawziin tiʃràbu ... ?
homma	çawziin yiʃràbu ...

3. howwa nifsu yitçallim <u>çàràbi</u>
    He is dying to learn <u>Arabic.</u>

ana	nifsi atçallim çàràbi
inta	nifsak titçallim çàràbi? itçallim
inti	nifsik titçallimi çàràbi? (yitçallim)
hiyya	nifsaha titçallim ... to learn

ihna	nifsina nitçallim ...
intu	nifsoku titçallimu çàràbi?
homma	nifsohom yitçallimu çàràbi

4. howwa laazim yiruuh iȿȿoġl

He must go to <u>work</u>.

ana	laazim àruuh iȿȿoġl
inta	laazim tiruuh iȿȿoġl
inti	laazim tiruuhi ... ràȧh (yiruuh)
hiyya	laazim tiruuh ... to go
ihna	laazim niruuh ...
intu	laazim tiruuhu ...
homma	laazim yiruuhu ...

5. howwa mafruud yiçmil ȿoġlu

He is supposed to do his work.

ana	màfruud açmil ȿoġli
inta	màfruud tiçmil ȿoġlak
inti	màfruud tiçmili ȿoġlik çamal (yiçmil)
hiyya	màfruud tiçmil ȿoġlaha to do
ihna	màfruud niçmil ȿoġlina
intu	màfruud tiçmilu ȿoġloku
homma	màfruud yiçmilu ȿoġlohom

6. howwa yimkin yisaafir bokrà

He might leave (travel) <u>tomorrow</u>.

ana	yimkin aȿaafir bokrà
inta	yimkin tisaafir bokrà? saafir
inti	yimkin tisafri bokrà? (yisaafir)
hiyya	yimkin tisaafir ... to travel
ihna	yimkin nisaafir ...
intu	yimkin tisafru bokrà?
homma	yimkin yisafru bokrà

7.   howwa momkin <u>yifuut çaleeha</u> (expression)

       He can (is capable of) <u>pick her up</u>. (pass by her)

ana	momkin afuut çaleeha	
inta	momkin tifuut çaleeha?	
inti	momkin tifuuti ...?	faat (çala)
hiyya	momkin tifuut çaleeha?	(yifuut)
ihna	momkin nifuut çaleeha	to pass (by)
intu	momkin tifuutu ...?	
homma	momkin yifuutu çaleeha	

Repeat the following in the above order without transcription:

1.   howwa gaayiz <u>yiigi</u> nnàhàrdà

2.   howwa <u>yiḥibb</u> <u>yaakol</u> <u>koosa</u>   (zuccini)

       howwa yiḥibb yaakol <u>bamia</u>   (okra)

3.   howwa yiçraf yitkallim <u>ingifiizi</u>   (English)

       howwa yiçràf yitkallim <u>faransaawi</u>   (French)

4.   howwa yi'dàr yiṣiil iṣṣàntà

Denying Desire, Probability, Possibility and Obligation

Negation of the Imperfect

    There is more than one way of negating a sentence which includes an imperfect verb. We will give you examples of these methods:

1.   In a sequence of two verbs, we negate the <u>first</u> verb. We do not touch the imperfect. It is only a helping verb.

    nizilt aṣtiri gazma
    manziltiṣ aṣtiri gazma

2. The following words will take "miʃ" in front of them. Again the imperfect verb itself remains untouched:

çaawiz áʃràb

miʃ çaawiz áʃràb

Here is a list:

laazim	miʃ laazim
màfruud	miʃ màfruud
dàruuri	miʃ dàruuri
çaawiz	miʃ çaawiz
momkin	miʃ momkin

3. Sentences that include <u>nifsi</u> will take "ma ___ ʃ." "ma ___ ʃ" will surround nifsi. The rule for words ending in C/CC/V applies here.

4. In responding to questions about <u>desire</u> or <u>capability</u> in the <u>negative</u>, we <u>negate the imperfect verb itself</u> by using "ma ___ ʃ":

tiçràf çàràbi

Do you know Arabic?

la', maçràfʃ çàràbi

No, I don't know Arabic.

Again, in this case the rule of words ending in C/CC/V applies.

TAPE IX/SIDE 2
Negation of the Imperfect

Please turn back to the transcriptions of Tape IX/SIDE 1. Work closely with them for the following drills. We will be using the same sentences for the drills on the negative. There will be some slight variations. You will be given directions on the tape. Before you begin, please review our grammatical notes.

TAPE IX/SIDE 2
Translate the Passage then Answer the Questions

(On tape--no transcriptions)

Expressing Facts, Habits and Progressive Actions

The Present Tense (bi + imperfect)

The prefix "bi" + the imperfect is the formula from which we obtain the present tense. Here are some examples:

howwa bi+yiruuh i$$oġl koll yoom

He goes to work every day.

hiyya bi+truuh i$$oġl koll yoom

She goes to work every day.

TAPE X/SIDE 1

Conjugation of "sihi"

Please Listen and Repeat

	sihi	to wake up
	perfect/(sihi)	imperfect/(yishà)

pronoun	prefix	naked imperfect
ana		b àshà badri
inta	bi	tishà "
inti	bi	tishi "
howwa	bi	yishà "
hiyya	bi	tishà "
ihna	bi	nishà "
intu	bi	tishu "
homma	bi	yishu "

When do we use the present tense, or the
bi+imperfect?

1.   When we are expressing a habit:

     koll yoom banaam issaaça xamsa

     Every day I sleep at 5:00 o'clock.

2.   When we are expressing a fact:

     howwa biyhibb màsr

     He likes Egypt.

3.   When we are expressing something in progress;
     something that is happening now, that has not yet
     finished:

     homma biyiɣràbu ɣaay dilwa'ti

     They are drinking tea now.

NOTE: When bi+imperfect is used for an action that
         is happening now it translates as a continuous
         (is drinking) rather than a simple present
         (drinks).

     The above are the usages of the bi+imperfect.
Sometimes it is the context that determines the usage of
this tense:

ana baakol

depending on	I eat	(fact)
the context	I eat	(habit)
it could mean	I am eating	(progressive- now)

The Present Tense (bi + imperfect)

Respond by using bi + imperfect.

1. howwa biynaam waxri
   He sleeps late.

ana	banaam waxri
inta	bitnaam ... ?
inti	bitnaami ... ?
hiyya	bitnaam
ihna	binnaam waxri
intu	bitnaamu
homma	biynaamu

   naam (yinaam)
   to sleep

2. kal? ...   la', biyaakol
   Did he eat ...   No, he's eating.

kalt? ...	la', baakol
kalti? ...	la', baakol
kalit? ...	la', bitaakol
kaltu? ...	la', binaakol
kalu? ...	la', biyaklu

   kal (yaakol)
   to eat

3. howwa biyistanna l'otobiis hina
   He waits for the bus here.   istanna (yistanna)

ana	bastanna l'otobiis hina
inta	bitistanna l'otobiis hina?
inti	bitistanni l'otobiis hina?
hiyya	bitistanna l'otobiis ...
ihna	binistanna l'otobiis ...
intu	bitistannu l'otobiis hina?

   to wait

4. howwa biyiṣtaġal baҫd isaaҫa ҫàṣàrà
   He works after ten o'clock.

ana	baɟtaġal baçd issaaça çàɟàrà
inta	bitiɟtaġal baçd issaaça çàɟàrà
inti	bitiɟtaġali .... ? iɟtaġal (yiɟtaġal)
hiyya	bitiɟtaġal .... ? to work
ihna	biniɟtaġal ....
intu	bitiɟtaġalu .... ?
homma	biyiɟtaġalu ....

5. howwa <u>leeh</u> biyiigi hina?

<u>Why</u> does he come here?

inta	leeh bitiigi hina?
inti	leeh bitiigi hina?
hiyya	leeh bitiigi hina?
ihna	leeh biniigi hina?
intu	leeh bitiigu hina?
homma	leeh biyiigu hina?

Negation of the Present Tense

The present tense (bi + imperfect) is negated by using
"miɟ" <u>in front of</u> the verb:

ana baɟtaġal

ana miɟ baɟtaġal

TAPE X/SIDE 1

Negation of the Present Tense

We will repeat the previous drill putting the sentences
in the <u>negative</u>. Please follow the directions on the
tape.

What Will Happen/What Will Not Happen

We use the naked imperfect together with the prefix (ha) to express things in the future: actions that have nȯt yet taken place.

Here is an example:

bȧruuh innaadi

I go to the club.

hȧrruuh innaadi

I will go to the club.

TAPE X/SIDE 2

Conjugation of "rȧȧh"

Listen and Repeat

	rȧȧh		to go	
	perfect/rȧȧh	–	imperfect/yiruuh	
ana	h	ȧruuh		
inta	ha	truuh		
inti	ha	truuhi	nnaadi	(club)
howwa	ha	yiruuh		
hiyya	ha	truuh		
ihna	ha	nruuh		
intu	ha	truuhu		

We will give you sentences in the past (perfect)
and others in the present (bi + imperfect). We will
ask you to make them future (ha + imperfect).

You should know the naked imperfect of the verbs in
the sentences to respond quickly. Please look up the
verbs before you begin your drills. They are all on
your verb list.

TAPE X/SIDE 2

The Future

Change the following to the future then translate the
new sentence:

1. howwa dafaç ilhisaab   (dafaç)

2. ihna dafaçna lhisaab   (dafaç)

3. hiyya çamalit ṣoġlaha   (çamal)

4. inta çamalt ṣoġlak?   (çamal)

5. homma fitru badri   (fitir)

6. ana fitirt badri   (fitir)

7. ihna nizilna lbalad   (nizil)

8. howwa nizil ilbalad   (nizil)

9. inti la'eeti ṣa"a?   (la'a)

10. hiyya la'et ṣa"a   (la'a)

11. ihna hatteena lfoluus filbank   (hatt)

12. ilba"aal baaç ilmahall   (baaç)

13. ana bàruuh innaadi   (ràåh)

14. howwa biyistanna lmodiir   (istanna)

15. ihna biniṣtiri beet   (iṣtara)

16. hiyya bitiddi Mohamed foluus   (idda)

17. ana bastanna lmodiir   (istanna)

18. inta bitruuh innaadi?   (ràåh)

146

19. inti biti¢tiri beet?   (i¢tara)

20. homma biyiddu Mohamed foluus   (idda)

Negation of the Future

Like the <u>present</u> (bi + imperfect) we add "mi¢" in front
of the verb.

TAPE X/SIDE 2

Negation of the Future

Negate the following:

1. hayidfaç ilhisaab?

    Will he pay the bill?

    la', mi¢ hayidfaç ilhisaab

2. hatidfaçu lhisaab?

    la', mi¢ hanidfaç ilhisaab

3. hatiçmil ¢oġlak?

    1', mi¢ haçmil ¢oġli

4. haylaa'u ¢a"a?

    la', mi¢ haylaa'u ¢a"a

5. ilba"aal haybiiç ilmahall?

    la', mi¢ haybiiç ilmahall

6. hàtruuhu nnaadi?

    la', mi¢ hànruuh innaadi

7. hatinzili lbalad?

    la', mi¢ <u>hanzil</u> ilbalad

8. hayistanna lmodiir?

    la', mi¢ hayistanna lmodiir

147

9. haništiri çàràbiyyà?

   la', miš haništiri çàràbiyyà

10. hatšuuf ilfilm?

    la', miš hašuuf ilfilm

Giving Orders

The Imperative

The imperative is the tense we use to make commands. It has one thing in common with the naked imperfect of the verb: the vowel. Here are some examples:

TAPE X/SIDE 2

Perfect, Imperfect and Imperative

Listen and Repeat

perfect	imperfect	imperative	
ràah	yiruuh	ruuh	(go)
naam	yinaam	naam	(sleep)
kal	yaakol	kol	(eat)
nizil	yinzil	inzil	(come down)
aam	yi'uum	uum	(get up)
fatah	yiftah	iftah	(open up)

If you know the imperfect tense you will be able to guess at the imperative and vice versa.

Orders are given to:

you	inta	(3rd m. s.)
you	inti	(3rd f. s.)
you	intu	(3rd pl.)

    Therefore the imperative exists with the three
above pronouns only. With the imperative we do not need
to repeat the personal pronouns (inta - inti - intu).
We begin the sentence with the verb in the imperative.

The imperative has a different form with each person.
This is the only way we can tell to whom the order is
being addressed. Here are some examples:

pronouns	ráàh	fatah	istanna
inta	ruuh	iftah	istanna
inti	ruuhi	iftahi	istanni
intu	ruuhu	iftahu	istannu

TAPE X/SIDE 2

The Imperative

We will give you the imperative with "inta." Please
supply "inti" and "intu":

1. kallim ilmodiir   talk to the manager

2. taçaala çandina   come to our place

3. oxrog bárrà   get out

4. itfáddál ʃaay   please have tea

5. haawil tiigi   try to come

6. istanna ʃwayya   wait a little

7. uul taani   say it again

8. ismaç kalaami   listen to my words

9. rodd çala ttilifoon   answer the phone

10. iʃtiri fakha   buy some fruit

11. idfaç ilhisaab   pay the cheque

12. haat boosa   give me a kiss

13. itlob iddoktor   call the doctor

14. istahamma bisorçà   take a bath quickly

15. xod foluusak   take your money

149

Negation of the Imperative

Like the perfect, the imperative is negated by
using "ma ____ ∅" around the verb itself. However, the
verb itself is not in the imperative form you have just
seen above. It is in the imperfect. What we are
actually doing is adding "ma ____ ∅" to the naked
imperfect verb with the three persons (inta - inti -
intu). Here are some examples:

imperative	negation of imperative	
	ma	imperfect ∅
ruuh	ma	truh ∅
ruuhi	ma	truhi i∅
ruuhu	ma	truhu u∅

Notice that the rule for words ending in C/CC/V
will also apply here when we add "ma ____ ∅."

TAPE X/SIDE 2

Negation of the Imperative

Give orders in the negative:

i∅tiri fakha

buy fruit

mati∅triii∅ fakha

don't buy fruit

1. kallim ilmodiir

    inta   matkallim∅ ilmodiir

    inti   matkallimii∅ ilmodiir

    intu   matkallimuu∅ ilmodiir

2. taçaala çandina (This verb exists only in
                imperative.)
                (Come to our place.)

	inta	mat giiʃ	çandina	geh (yigi)	to come
	inti	matgiiʃ	çandina		
	intu	matguuʃ	çandina		

3. ismaç kalaamu

	inta	matismaçʃ	kalaamu
	inti	matismaçiiʃ	kalaamu
	intu	matismaçuuʃ	kalaamu

4. rodd çalayya   (answer me)

	inta	matroddiʃ	çalayya
	inti	matroddiiʃ	çalayya
	intu	matrodduuʃ	çalayya

5. itlob iddoktoor

	inta	matitlobʃ	iddoktoor
	inti	matitlobiiʃ	iddoktoor
	intu	matitlobuuʃ	iddoktoor

TAPE X/SIDE 2

Translation Quiz

Answers to Translation:

1. nimt badri
2. banaam badri
3. hanaam badri
4. naam badri
5. miʃ haynaam badri
6. manamʃ badri
7. miʃ hatnaam badri
8. miʃ haynaamu badri

151

9. hatnaam badri?

10. hatnaam <u>imta</u>?　(when)

11. hatruuh innaadi

12. rohna nnaadi

13. måtrohş innaadi

14. fåkkår fil måwduuҫ

15. hanfåkkår fil måwduuҫ

16. båfåkkår fil måwduuҫ

17. biyiştaġalu koll yoom

18. iştaġalit imbaarih

19. hayiştaġal maҫaaya

20. hott işşåntå fil'oodå

21. håhott işşåntå fil'oodå

Things We <u>Used</u> to Do/Things We Had the Intention of Doing

<u>Two Uses of "kaan" with the Verbal Sentence</u>

When "<u>kaan</u>" is used with the nominal sentence, the whole structure becomes <u>past</u>. For example:

Mohamed mawguud   Mohamed is (present) here.

Mohamed <u>kaan</u> mawguud   Mohamed <u>was</u> (present) here.

When "<u>kaan</u>" is used with verbal sentences it establishes more complex tenses. We will concentrate here on the use of "<u>kaan</u>" with <u>two tenses</u> only: the <u>present</u> (bi + imperfect) and the <u>future</u> (ha + imperfect). Special attention is given to these two tenses because they are the most commonly used.

1.   <u>"kaan" With the Present Tense:</u>

    kaan biyruuh

    kaanit bitruuh

    (kaan + bi + imperfect).

2.   <u>"kaan" With the Future Tense:</u>

    kaan hayruuh

    kaanit hatruuh

    (kaan + ha + imperfect).

1.   <u>"kaan" With the Present Tense:</u>

    When kaan is used with the present it allows us to say:

    a.   "I <u>used</u> to do"

or   b.   "I <u>was doing</u>" depending on the <u>context</u>:

153

Here are some examples:

Present:

ana bàruuh innaadi   I go to the club.

"kaan" + present:

ana kont bàruuh innaadi   I used to go to
                            the club.

present:

howwa biyaakol kwayyis   He eats well.

"kaan" + present:

howwa kaan biyaakol kwayyis He used to eat
                            well.

progressive present (bi + imperfect):

howwa biyiȿràb   He is drinking.

"kaan" + progressive present:

howwa kaan biyiȿràb   He was drinking.

2. "kaan" With the Future:

When kaan is used with the future it allows
us to say: "I was going to do ..." It expresses
an intention that remains to be realized.

hàruuh innaadi   I will go to the club.
kont hàruuh innaadi   I was going to go to the
                          club.

haniçmil ȿoġlina   We will do our work.
konna haniçmil ȿoġlina   We were going to do our
                          work.

<u>"kaan" With the Verbal Sentence</u>:

<u>Add "kaan" then Translate the New Sentence</u>:

At this stage of the course we would like you to
<u>listen</u> to the tape only. There will be no transcribed
material for you. You already know the verb <u>"kaan."</u>
You also know the two tenses: <u>present</u> and <u>future</u>. The
sentences used on this tape are sentences you have seen
before.

Things We Are Still Doing/ Things We Have Just Done

<u>The Active Participle</u>

The <u>verb</u> expresses an <u>action</u>.

The <u>active participle</u> describes <u>the state of the</u>
<u>doer of that action</u>. Here is an example:

| verb | ana <u>fihimt</u> | I understood |
| active participle | ana <u>faahim</u> | I understand |

The difference between the first sentence which
includes the perfect, and the second, which includes an
active participle <u>derived</u> from the same <u>root</u> as the verb
in the first sentence, is that:

1.   The verb expresses an <u>action</u>.

2.   The active participle expresses the <u>state</u> of the
     doer of that action rather than the <u>action</u> itself.

The active participle derives from a basic <u>root</u>.
It shares the basic meaning of all patterns derived from
that same root.

Fortunately, the active participle has a regular pattern. Here are some examples:

Verb Form I	Act. part.	Other Verbs	Act. part.
çirif (to know)	çaarif	iştara (to buy)	miştiri
fihim (to understand)	faahim	istanna (to wait)	mistanni

Verb Form I	Act. part.	Other Verbs	Act. part.
xaaf (to fear)	xaayif	itkallim (to speak)	mitkallim
ŝaaf (to see)	/aayif	itnaa'iŝ (discuss)	mitnaa'iŝ
habb (to love)	haabib	saafir (travel)	misaafir
bȧss (to look)	bȧȧsis	saaçid (to help)	misaaçid
naam (to sleep)	naayim	aabil (to meet)	mi'aabil
nisi (to forget)	naasi	sallim (to greet)	misallim
miŝi (to leave)	maaŝi	dȧyyȧç (to ˙lose)	midȧyyȧç

Use of the Active Participle:

1. The active participle <u>describes a state</u>.

2. That state can be anywhere along a linear axis-- past, present or future.

3. Some active participles can only describe <u>past states</u>, while others can describe present or future states, depending on the meaning of the verb.

4. We can divide verbs into three categories:

    a. Verbs of <u>motion</u>
    b. Verbs of <u>state</u>
    c. Verbs <u>"to do"</u>

The active participle will connote past, present or future <u>states</u> depending on which category the verb from which it derives belongs to.

a.   <u>Verbs of Motion</u>

When we speak of <u>motion</u> we really mean <u>moving oneself</u> from one place to the other. Here are some examples:

xàràg	to go out
daxal	to enter
tiliç	to go up
nizil	to go down

This group of verbs is limited. <u>Active participles that derive from verbs of <u>motion</u> connote a present state, or a future state</u>, depending on the context:

xàràg   to go out

active participle   xaarig

<u>Past Tense:</u>

ana xàràgt baçd iddohr   I went out in the afternoon.

<u>Present Tense:</u>

ana bàxrog baçd iddohr   I go out in the afternoon.

Active Participle:

ana <u>xaarig</u> baçd iddohr   I am going out in the
afternoon.

Future Tense:

ana <u>hȧxrog</u> baçd iddohr   I will go out in the
afternoon.

    Active participles of verbs of motion resemble the
verb in the future except that the verb stresses <u>action</u>
while the participle describes a <u>state</u>.

b.   Verbs of State

    When we speak of <u>state</u>, we mean an action that is
very long; that has a <u>duration</u> which extends beyond the
immediate present either in the past or in the future.

Consider some examples of verbs of state:

Verb	Active Participle
çirif (to know)	çaarif
xaaf (to fear)	xaayif
fihim (to understand)	faahim
istanna (to wait)	mistanni

    These are all <u>verbs of state</u>. The active
participle derived from verbs of state connotes a <u>state
in the present</u>:

ana <u>çaarif</u>   I <u>know</u>

howwa faahim   he <u>understands</u>

c.   Verbs "to do"

    Unlike verbs of motion, "to do" verbs connote doing
things, <u>not</u> displacing oneself from one place to the
other. Active participles that derive from "to do"

158

verbs all connote a <u>state in the past</u>. Here are some examples:

ana ¢aarib ¢aay   I <u>drank</u> tea.

howwa <u>waakil</u> lahma   He ate meat.

These active participles seem to function like the verb in the past tense. They do, indeed, come quite close. However, the participle describes <u>a state</u> while the verb expresses an <u>action</u>.

The active participle has three forms: masculine, feminine, and plural.

The following is a table which includes:

1. The verb in the past tense.
2. The meaning of the verb in English.
3. The masculine singular form of the active participle (used for "I," "you," "he").
4. The category of the verb (motion, state, or "to do").
5. The feminine singular form of the active participle (used for "I," "you," "she").
6. The plural form of the active participle (used for "we," "you," "they").

TAPE XI/SIDE 1

<u>The Active Participle</u>

<u>Please Listen and Repeat</u>

(On tape - no transcriptions)

VERB	MEANING	ACT. PART.	CATEGORY	FEMININE	PLURAL
sikin	to reside	saakin	Verbs of	sakna	sakniin
fihim	to understand	faahim	STATE	fahma	fahmiin
simiç	to hear	saamiç	participle	samça	samçiin
sihi ..	to awaken	sàahi ..	connotes	sàhyà ..	sàhyiin ..
çaaz	to want	çaawiz	present	çawza	çawziin
çirif	to know	çaarif	state	çarfa	çarfiin
naam	to sleep	naayim		nayma	naymiin
çaaş	to live	çaayiş		çayşa	çayşiin
şaaf	to see	şaayif		şayfa	şayfiin
libis	to wear	laabis		labsa	labsiin
istanna	to wait	mistanni		mistanniyya	mistanniyiin
dafaç	to pay	daafiç	Verbs	dafça	dafçiin
axad	to take	waaxid	"to do"	waxda	waxdiin

160

VERB	MEANING	ACT. PART.	CATEGORY	FEMININE	PLURAL
akal	to eat	waakil	participle	wakla	wakliin
çamal	to do	çaamil	connotes	çamla	çamliin
ʃirib	to drink	ʃaarib	accomplished	ʃarba	ʃarbiin
talab.	to order	taalib.	state	talba.	talbiin.
idda	to give	middi		middiyya	midiyiin
nisi	to forget	naasi		nasya	nasyiin
fatah.	to open	faatih.		fatha.	fathiin.
istahamma.	to shower	mistahammi.		mistahammiyya	mistahammiyiin.
nizil	to go down	naazil	Verbs of	nazla	nazliin
xárág	to go out	xaarig	MOTION	xarga	xargiin
daxal	to enter	daaxil	participle	daxla	daxliin
ráàh.	to go	ráàyih.	connotes	ráyhà.	ráyhiin
miʃi	to leave; to walk	maaʃi	present or future state	maʃya	maʃyiin

TAPE XI/SIDE 1

The Active Participle

Translation

Translate the following sentences into Arabic,
using the active participle and not the verb. Then give
the feminine and plural forms with necessary changes
according to the directions given on tape:

1. He lives in Egypt. (m.s.)

2. She lives in France.   çaaʂ

3. We live in the USA.

4. I want a room, please. (f.s.)

5. He wants the contract.   çaaz

6. Are you sleeping? (m.s.)

7. Are you sleeping? (f.s.)   naam

8. I drank tea. (m.s.)

9. She drank tea.   ʂirib

10. We drank coffee.

11. I did my work. (m.s.)

12. She did her work.   çamal

13. They did their work.

14. He bought a new car.

15. She bought a big apartment.   iʂtara

16. We bought many things.

17. I am going downtown.

18. She is going downtown.   nizil

19. Are you going downtown? (pl.)

20. I am going home. (f.s.)

21. He is going home now.   ràwwàh

22. We are going home tomorrow.

162

23. Mohamed is going up the <u>stairs</u>. (issillim)

24. She is going up to Alexandria.

25. They are going upstairs.

TAPE XI/SIDE 1

The Active Participle

Form sentences using the active participle from the following; then translate the new sentence into English.

ana - libis - badla

ana laabis badla   I am wearing a suit.

1. hiyya - libis - fostaan

2. ihna - xàràg - billeel

3. howwa - xàràg - maçaaya

4. inti - daxal - il'oodà?

5. inta - rààh - feen?

6. homma - fihim - koll haaga

7. ana - çirif - <u>ilhikaaya</u> (story)

8. hiyya - nizil - ilbalad

9. ihna - ʃirib - ʃaay

"Lissa" and the Active Participle

"Lissa" could mean:

1. just
2. yet
3. still

  It depends on the <u>context</u> and the <u>category</u> to which the active participle belongs.

1. **"Lissa"   just:**

It is used with active participles of verbs of
motion and verbs "to do"

Verbs of Motion:

Mohamed xaarig	Mohamed is going out.
Mohamed <u>lissa</u> xaarig	Mohamed has <u>just</u> gone out.

Verbs "to do"

ana mitnaa'i∮ maça Nadia	I argued with Nadia.
ana <u>lissa</u> mitnaa'i∮ maça Nadia	I have <u>just</u> argued with Nadia.

Notice that "<u>lissa</u>" with active participles of
verbs of motion changes the meaning of the
participle in the sentence. See examples above.

2. **"Lissa"   still:**

"Lissa" with participles of <u>verbs of state</u> gives us
"still":

Mohamed naayim	Mohamed is sleeping.
Mohamed <u>lissa</u> naayim	Mohamed is <u>still</u> sleeping.

TAPE XI/SIDE 1

<u>"Lissa" and the Active Participle</u>

<u>Use "lissa" with the Following, then Translate the
Sentence:</u>

1. ana waakil

2. ihna ∮arbiin

3. Mona nayma

4. homma nazliin

5. hiyya mistanniyya

6. inta mistahammi?

7. intu <u>gayyiin</u>?   (coming)

8. inti gayya?

9. inta <u>faakir</u>?   (remember)

10. ana mistiriyya fostaan

TAPE XI/SIDE 1

<u>Review Drills</u>

<u>Follow the Directions on the tape.</u>

What Did He Give to You

Direct and Indirect Object Suffixes

There are two kinds of objects: direct and indirect.

1.   The <u>direct object</u> answers the question "who" or
     "what." Here is an example:

     We put <u>the bag</u>.

     <u>What</u> did we put?

     We saw <u>the girl</u>.

     <u>Who</u> did we see?

     In Egyptian Arabic:

     "what" is   "eeh"

     "who" is   "miin"

     So, the <u>direct object</u> in Arabic answers the
     question "eeh?" or "miin?". Here are some
     examples:

     hatteena <u>ʃʃánta</u>
     We put the bag.

     hatteena <u>eeh</u>?

     ʃofna <u>lbint</u>

     We saw the girl.

     ʃofna <u>miin</u>?

2.   The <u>indirect object</u> answers the questions: "to
     whom" or "for whom." Here are some examples:

     We gave the money to Nadia.

We gave <u>what</u>?

the money   (direct object)

<u>To whom</u> did we give the money?

We gave the money <u>to Nadia</u>. (indirect)

In Egyptian Arabic:

"to whom"

"for whom"   is   "limiin"

So, the <u>indirect object</u> in Arabic answers the
question "limiin." Here are some examples:

iddeena lfoluus <u>liNadia</u>?

iddeena <u>eeh</u>?

ilfoluus   (direct object)

iddeena lfoluus <u>limiin</u>?

<u>liNadia</u>   (indirect object)

Sometimes when we do not wish to repeat the name of
a person we use a pronoun:

We saw <u>him</u>.
We saw <u>her</u>.

We gave <u>her</u> the money
We gave <u>them</u> the money.

The same is done in Arabic except that the pronoun
<u>is</u> added to the verb as a <u>suffix</u>, thus becoming the
object. Here are some examples:

$ofn<u>aah</u> $ofna + ah

We saw <u>him</u>.   direct

$ofn<u>aha</u> $ofna + aha   <u>$ofna miin</u>

We saw <u>her</u>.

iddena<u>lha</u>   iddeena + lha

We gave <u>her</u> the money.

168

iddena<u>lhom</u>   iddeena + lohom

We gave <u>them</u> the money.

    The process of adding the pronominal suffix object
(direct or indirect) to the verb is highly complex on
the phonetic plane. Many changes occur once we merge
the separate verb with the separate suffix pronoun. We
will provide you with two tables. One shows the
pronominal suffix as direct object and the other shows
the pronominal suffix used as an indirect object.
Familiarize yourself with the <u>sounds</u>. We do not wish to
burden you with phonetic rules. Keep in mind the C/ CC/
V rule while doing the drills. It will help you explain
why some vowels are shortened, some dropped, and others
are lengthened.

TAPE XI/SIDE 2

<u>Direct Object Suffixes</u>

<u>Please Listen and Repeat</u>

šaal   to carry
perfect šaal   imperfect/ yišiil

	šal	ni		carried <u>me</u>
	šaal	ak		carried <u>you</u>
howwa	šaal	ik	he	carried <u>you</u>
	šaal	u		carried <u>him</u>
	šal	ha		carried <u>her</u>
	šal	na		carried <u>us</u>
howwa	šal	ku	he	carried <u>you</u>
	šal	hom		carried <u>them</u>

habb   to like
 .

perfect/habb		imperfect/yihibb		
	habb	ini		liked me
	habb	ak		liked you
	habb	ik		liked you
howwa	habb	u	he	liked him
	habb	aha		liked her
	habb	ina		liked us
	habb	oku		liked you
	habb	ohom		liked them

la'a   to find

perfect/la'a   imperfect/yilaa'i

	la'a	ani		found me
	la'a	ak		found you
	la'a	ak<u>i</u>		found you
howwa	la'a	ah	he	found him
	la'a	aha		found her
	la'a	ana		found us
	la'a	aku		found you
	la'a	ahom		found them

Indirect Object Suffixes

aal   to tell

perfect/aal   imperfect/yi'uul

	al	li	told me
	al	lak	told you
howwa	al	lik	told you

aal limiin?	al	lu	he	told him
	al	laha	he	told her
	al	lina		told us
	al	loku		told you
	al	lohom		told them

bàss to look at ...
perfect/bàss imperfect/yibòss
(remember CCC)

	bàss	ili		looked at me
	bàss	ilak		looked at you
howwa	bàss	ilik	he	looked at you
bàss limiin?	bàss	ilu		looked at him
	bàss	ilha		looked at her
	bàss	ilna		looked at us
	bàss	ilku		looked at you
	bàss	ilhom		looked at them

haka to tell (a story)
ṗerfect/haka imperfect/yihki
(rememberŕ <u>V</u> ending)

	haka	ali		recounted
to me				
	haka	alak		recounted to you
	haka	alik		recounted to you
howwa	haka	alu	he	recounted to him
	haka	lha		recounted to her
haka limiin?	haka	lna		recounted to us
	haka	lku		recounted to you

haka	lhom	recounted to them

TAPE XI/SIDE 2

Indirect Object Suffixes

Translate the Following into Arabic (on tape)

TAPE XI/SIDE 2

Review Drills

Follow the Instructions on the Tape.

Almost Everything You Want to Say

Beyond the Simple Sentence

So far we have really been dealing with the simple sentence. The structures we have covered are basic. All the verbal sentences we have heard on tape contained one verb only. Now we will introduce more complex structures.

1.   How do we say:

The girl who is upstairs.

The chair that is in the room.

The car which I bought.

"illi" is the means by which we can say all these things. While English uses "which," "that" for

172

things, and "who" for people, Arabic uses "illi" only. Let us translate the sentences above.

Ilbint illi foo'

Ikkorsi lli fil'oodå

Ilçåråbiyyå lli ¢taritha

NOTE: "illi" is preceeded by a noun with a definite article. For the purposes of this course, we will remain at this level.

2. How do we say:

I saw him while I was walking.

They came when she was eating.

"we" is the means by which we can say all this. This is not the "we" that you already know; it is not "and." It is the adverbial "we." Again "we" like "illi" is a constant. It does not change. Let us translate the sentences above.

¢oftu wana maa¢i

gom we hiyya bitaakol

3. How do you say:

I ate before he arrived.

I ate as soon as he arrived.

I ate after he arrived.

I ate until he arrived.

I ate when he arrived.

All the above are a combination of "_____ + ma."

before	abl ma
as soon as	awwil ma
after	baçd ma
until	liĝaayit ma
	lihadd ma
when	lamma

173

4. How do you say:

We will go out _if_ he comes.

She will eat _if_ they eat.

"iza" and "law" are the means by which we express the conditional. Again, they do not change. Let us translate the sentences above. You can use "iza" and "law" alternately in Egyptian Arabic.

hanoxrog iza geh.
.

hataakol law kalu.
.

5. How do you say:

I know _that you_ are here.

She suspects _that he_ is inside.

I told him _that she_ is outside.

"inn" is the means by which we express the nominal clause introduced by "that." "inn" takes suffix pronouns. Let us first translate the sentences, then we will give you a table:

ana ҫaarif innak hina.

hiyya ẓakka innu gowwa.

oltilu innaha barra.

"inn" with the Suffixes

inni	that I ...
innak	that you ...
innik	that you ...
innu	that he ...
innaha	that she ...
innina	that we ...
innoku	that you ...
innohom	that they ...

174

TAPE XI/SIDE 2

Beyond the Simple Sentence

There will be no transcriptions. Follow the
directions on tape for the drills on this section.

Self-Testing

Texts and Dialogues

TAPE XII/SIDE 1

UNIT ONE

Do this section after you have finished Unit I of the text. Memorize the following dialogue, then translate it into English. Our translation will be on the next page. Check your work against the model answers. Now listen and repeat:

Sally   —   såbååh ilxeer!

George   —   såbååh innuur. inti Nancy?

Sally   —   la', ana Sally. winta miin?

George   —   ana George. ahlan ya Sally! izzayyik?

Sally   —   ilhamdu-li-llaah, kwayisa. izzayyak inta?

George   —   wallaahi, miʃ båttåål. Sally, inti min Faransa, miʃ kida?

Sally   —   la' ya George, ana min Amriika. ana tååliba hina fi måsr.

George   —   wana Kamaan!

Sally   —   inta måsri?

George   —   la' ana kamaan Amrikaani!

Sally   —   miʃ maç'uul!

NEW WORDS

såbååh ilxeer   Good morning.

sȧbȧȧh innuur	Response to sabaah ilxeer.
ahlan	Hello, welcome, hi!
izzayyak (m.)	
izzayyik (f.)	How are you?
kwayyis (m.)	
kwayyisa (f.)	Good, fine OK . . . etc.
Ilhamdu-li-laah	Thanks be to God. (Response to izzayyak.)
wallaahi	By God!
miɬ bȧttȧȧl	Not so bad, so-so.
ya	Vocative particle used to call someone.
tȧȧlib (m. s.)	
tȧȧlibȧ (f. s.)	student
tollȧȧb/tȧlȧbȧ (pl.)	
kamaan	more, also, another
mȧsri (m. s.)	
mȧsriyyȧ (f. s.)	Egyptian
mȧsriyyiin (pl.)	
amrikaani (m. s.)	
amrikaniyya (f. s.)	American
amrikaan (pl.)	
miɬ maç'uul	incredible, unbelievable

TRANSLATION OF THE DIALOGUE

Sally	—	Good morning!
George	—	Good morning, are you Nancy?
Sally	—	No, I am Sally. And who are you?
George	—	I am George. Hello Sally, how are you?
Sally	—	I'm fine, thanks be to God! How are you?

178

George	–	Well, so-so! Sally, are you from France?
Sally	–	No, George, I am from the USA. I am a student here in Egypt.
George	–	So am I!
Sally	–	Are you Egyptian?
George	–	No, I also am American.
Sally	–	Incredible!

* *   *   *   *   *   *   *   *   *

TAPE XII/SIDE 1

UNIT TWO

Do this section after you have finished Unit II of the text. Memorize the following dialogue, then translate it into English. Our translation will appear on the next page. Check your work against the model answers. Now listen and repeat:

George	–	eeh da ya Sally?
Sally	–	Da kitaab çan màsr.
George	–	ikkitaab da gdiid?
Sally	–	la', ikkitaab da adiim ya George.
George	–	yàtàrà, saçb?
Sally	–	la', da sahl xààlis!
George	–	eeh màwduuç ikkitaab?
Sally	–	issiyaasa, wil'qtisààd ilmàsri.
George	–	inti ʃàtrà awi ya Sally! ikkitaab da ġaali?
Sally	–	yaçni, noss noss. bass, da ktaab mohimm. itfàddàl!
George	–	motaʃakkir awi ya Sally!
Sally	–	ilçafw!

NEW WORDS

çan	about
yàtàrà	I wonder. (It is used at the beginning of a sentence. It is invariable.)
issiyaasa	politics
il'qtisààd	economics
yaçni	that is to say; in other words; well
bass	but; enough; only (comes at the end of a sentence)
itfàddàl (m. s.)	
itfàddàli (f. s.)	a polite gesture of offering
itfàddàlu (pl.)	something to someone.
motaʃakkir (m. s.)	
motaʃakkira (f. s.)	thank you
motaʃakkiriin (pl.)	
ilçafw	you're welcome. Don't mention it.

TRANSLATION OF THE DIALOGUE

George	–	What is this, Sally?
Sally	–	This is a book about Egypt.
George	–	Is this book new?
Sally	–	No, this book is old, George.
George	–	I wonder, is it difficult?
Sally	–	No, very easy!
George	–	What is the subject of the book?
Sally	–	Egyptian politics and economics.
George	–	You are very clever, Sally! Is this book expensive?
Sally	–	Well, so-so! But it is very important! Here ...

180

```
George     -    Thank you very much, Sally!

Sally      -    Don't mention it.

          *    *    *    *    *    *    *    *    *


TAPE XII/SIDE 1

UNIT THREE

Do this section after you have finished Unit III of the
text.  Memorize the following dialogue, then translate
it into English.  Our translation will appear on the
next page.  Check your work against the model answers.
Now listen and repeat:
```

Sally   -   ʂa''itak feen ya George?

George   -   ʂa''iti fi wist ilbalad, laakin
              maktabi bҫiid ʂowayya, winti?

Sally   -   ana sakna fbeet kibiir. ʂoġli kamaan
              filbeet da! yaҫni maktab ilmodiir
              filbeet! laakin ilbeet kibiir awi,
              wilmakaatib biҫiida.

George   -   Sally, momkin nimrit tilifoonik, min
              fȧdlik?

Sally   -   tȧbҫan! ahe nimrit tilifooni. ana
              mawguuda, koll yoom issobh
              filmaktab.

George   -   motaʂakkir! Ҫala fikra ya Sally,
              fostaanik hilw awi! da min hina?

Sally   -   aywa min hina. wi kamaan rixiis awi!
              inta ҫaawiz fostaan ҫaʂaan oxtak?

George   -   aywa!

Sally   -   ilmaḥall da kwayyis awi!....George,

ana gaçaana giddan!

George   -   wana kamaan! yàllà biina çalmàtçàm!

NEW WORDS

wist ilbalad	downtown
laakin	but, however
biçiid (m. s.)	
biçiida (f. s.)	far
boçaad (pl.)	
ʂowayya	a little bit of...
saakin (m. s.)	
sakna (f. s.)	to live in a place, to dwell,
sakniin (pl.)	to reside.
momkin	is it possible, it is possible
mawguud (m. s.)	
mawguuda (f. s.)	to be present, to be there
mawgudiin (pl.)	
tàbçàn	of course
issobh	in the morning
çala fikra	by the way
koll yoom	every day
hina	here
hinaak	there
çaawiz (m. s.)	
çawza (f. s.)	to want
çawziin (pl.)	
çaʂaan	for, because
mahall/mahallaat	shop, place

gaçaan (m. s.)

gaçaana (f. s.)   hungry

gaçaniin (pl.)

yållå biina çala...   let's go to

måtçåm/måtååçim   restaurant

TRANSLATION OF THE DIALOGUE

Sally   —   Where is your apartment, George?

George   —   My apartment is downtown, but my office
              is a little bit farther. And you?

Sally   —   I live in a big house. My work is also
              in that house. That is to say, the
              director's office is in the house.
              But the house is very big, and the
              offices are far.

George   —   Sally, may I have your phone number,
              please?

Sally   —   Of course! Here is my phone number. I
              am in the office every day in the
              morning.

George   —   Thank you! By the way, Sally, your
              dress is very pretty. Is it from here?

Sally   —   Yes, it is from here. It is also very
              cheap. Do you want a dress for your
              sister?

George   —   Yes.

Sally   —   This shop is very good. George, I am
              very hungry.

George   —   Me too! Let's go to the restaurant.

              *   *   *   *   *   *   *   *

UNIT FOUR

Do this section after you have finished Unit IV.
Memorize the following dialogue, then translate it into
English. Our translation will appear on the next page.
Check your work against the model answers. Now listen
and repeat:

George   -   aloo! sȧbȧȧh ilxeer ya Sally!

Sally   -   ahlan! izzayyak ya George?

George   -   ilhamdu-li-llaah! Sally, ihna
               çandina maçaad innahȧrdȧ, mi$ kida?

Sally   -   aywa! ana fakra.

George   -   çaawiz ilçinwaan bitaaçik, min fȧdlik.

Sally   -   ilbeet oddaam mȧhȧttit il'ȧtr, fi$$aariç
               bitaaç iggamça. lokȧndit ilHilton
               gambina çala $$imaal. ilbeet nimra
               waahid. sahl awi! maçaak çȧrȧbiyyȧ,
               mi$ kida?

George   -   aywa, tȧbçan. mota$akkir ya Sally.
               maça ssalaama.

Sally   -   allȧȧh yisallimak!

. . . .

Sally   -   ȧhlan George! aho beeti! ilmaktab
               bitaaçi taht, we $''iti foo'.

George   -   di haaga gamiila awi!

Sally   -   da ssaloon, we di odt issofrȧ, we çandi
               oodit noom wahda bass!

George   -   di $a''a hilwa awi! yȧtȧrȧ, mafruu$a?

Sally   -   la', koll ilçaf$ btaaça ana....

NEW WORDS

aloo	hello (on the phone)
faakir (m. s.)	
fakra (f. s.)	to remember
fakriin (pl.)	
çinwaan/çanawiin	address
måhåttå/måhåttååt	station
åtr/otorå	train
gamça/gamçaat	university
ǵimaal	left
yimiin	right
waahid (m. s.)	
wahda (f. s.)	one
maça ssalaama	goodbye (lit., with protection)
ållååh yisallimak	response to "maça ssalaama" goodbye "may God protect you"
saloon	formal living room
odt issofra	dining room
oodit noom	bedroom
mafruuǵa	furnished
ilçafǵ	the furniture

TRANSLATION OF THE DIALOGUE

George — Hello! Good morning Sally!

Sally — Hi! How are you George?

George — Fine, thanks be to God! Sally, we have an appointment today, right?

Sally — Yes, I remember!

George — I want your address, please.

Sally — The house is in front of the train station, on the university street. The

		Hilton hotel is next to us on the left. The house is number one. It's very easy! You have a car, right?
George	–	Yes, of course! Thank you Sally. Goodbye!
Sally	–	Goodbye!

. . . .

Sally	–	Hello George! Here's my house! My office is downstairs and my apartment is upstairs.
George	–	This is wonderful!
Sally	–	This is the livingroom, this is the diningroom, and I have one bedroom only.
George	–	This is a very nice apartment. I wonder, is it furnished?
Sally	–	No, all the furniture is mine.

*   *   *   *   *   *   *   *   *

TAPE XII/SIDE 1

UNIT FIVE

Do this section after you have finished Unit V of the text. Memorize the following dialogue, then translate it into English. Our translation will appear on the next page. Check your work against the model answers. Now listen and repeat:

Sally	–	isaaça kaam dilwa'ti, ya George?
George	–	isaaça hawaali sitta wnoss.
Sally	–	çaawiz haaga missuu'?
George	–	la', motaşakkir. maçaaki fluus kifaaya?
Sally	–	aywa, ana çawza hagaat kitiir. fiih ba''aal kwayyis hina?

George   –   aywa, wàrà ilbeet çala tool.   inti
              çarfa ṣṣaariç ilwaasiç bitaaç iggamça?
              ilba''aal da hinaak çala nnàsyà.
Sally   –   tàyyib, ana maṣya.
George   –   ana çandi ṣoġl dilwa'ti. webaçd kida,
              il'akl btaaçik ilmomtaaz!
Sally   –   Innàhàrdà ana taçbaana ṣwayya.
George   –   maçleṣṣ! ana tàbbààx haayil! ilçaṣa
              ssaaça tisça, in ṣaa' àllààh.
Sally   –   aywa, in ṣaa' àllààh!

NEW WORDS

issuu'	the market
kifaaya	enough
çala tool	immediately, straight ahead
çaarif (m. s.)	
çarfa (f. s.)	to know
çarfiin (pl.)	
çala nnàsyà	on the corner
tàyyib	OK
maaṣi (m. s.)	
maṣya (f. s.)	to leave
maṣyiin (pl.)	
momtaaz	excellent
maçleṣṣ	no problem
tàbbààx	a cook
haayil	great, outstanding
çaṣa	dinner
in saa' àllààh	if God wills it

187

TRANSLATION OF THE DIALOGUE

Sally	-	What time is it now, George?
George	-	It's around six thirty.
Sally	-	Do you want something from the market?
George	-	No, thank you. Do you have enough money?
Sally	-	Yes. I want many things! Is there a good grocer here?
George	-	Yes, immediately behind the house. You know the wide university street? The grocer is on the corner, over there.
Sally	-	OK. I'm leaving.
George	-	I have work now, but after that, your excellent food!
Sally	-	I am a bit tired today.
George	-	No problem! I'm a great cook. Dinner is at nine, in ǰaa' allaah!
Sally	-	In ǰaa' allaah (if God wills it).

* * * * * * * * *

TAPE XII/SIDE 1

UNIT SIX

Do this section after you have finished Unit VI.
Memorize the following dialogue, then translate it into
English. Our translation will appear on the next page.
Check your work against the model answers. Now listen
and repeat:

Sally	-	xàlààs! maçandiiǰ foluus xàális!
George	-	miǰmohimm. ittallaaga malyaana.
Sally	-	miǰ malyaana awi!
George	-	leeh? miǰ fiih xodàár?
Sally	-	la', mafiiǰ xodàár!

George   -   çandina fakha?

Sally   -   la', maçandinnaş fakha!

George   -   ġariiba! ommåål fiih eeh?

Sally   -   mafiiş haaga! issuu' kaan fåådi! makanş
               fiih wala mahall faatih! laakin kaan
               fiih okazyoon çala şonåt fi mahall
               oråyyib min hina...ahe şåntiti
               ggidiida! hilwa?

George   -   hilwa awi, bass da miş akl!

Sally   -   miş mohimm! ana xålåås miş gaçaana!

George   -   Bass ana gaçaan!

Sally   -   fiih şwayyit akl fittallaaga.

George   -   la' ittallaaga mafihaaş haaga!

Sally   -   tåyyib, çaawiz çeeş we gibna?

George   -   la', miş çaawiz, motaşakkir! tisbåhi
               çala xeer... ana maaşi!

Sally   -   winta min ahlu!

NEW WORDS

xålåås   finished

xodåår   vegetables

fakha   fruits

ġariiba   strange

ommåål   so?

wala mahall   not a single shop
faatih (m. s.)
fatha (f. s.)   open
fathiin (pl.)
okazyoon   a sale

oràyyib min hina	near by, close by
çeeş	bread
gibna	cheese
tisbàh cala xeer	good night
winta min ahlu	response to "tisbah cala xeer"

TRANSLATION OF DIALOGUE

Sally	–	Finished! I don't have any money!
George	–	No problem! The fridge is full.
Sally	–	Not very full!
George	–	Why? Aren't there any vegetables?
Sally	–	No, there aren't any vegetables!
George	–	Do we have fruit?
Sally	–	No, we don't have any fruit!
George	–	Strange! So what is there?
Sally	–	Nothing! The market was empty! There wasn't one single shop open! But there was a sale on handbags in a shop nearby .... Here's my new handbag! Pretty?
George	–	Very nice, but it isn't food!
Sally	–	So what! I'm not hungry anymore!
George	–	But I am hungry!
Sally	–	There is some food in the fridge.
George	–	No, there's nothing in the fridge!
Sally	–	OK. Do you want bread and cheese?
George	–	No I don't, thank you. Good night. I'm leaving.
Sally	–	Good night!

* * * * * * * * *

UNIT EIGHT

Do this section after you have finished Units VII &
VIII. Memorize the following passage. Start the same
passage once using "iḥna," and then "hiyya" and make all
the necessary changes. Check your answers against the
verb list in Units VII & VIII of the text. Now listen
and repeat:

Imbaarih la'eet ẓa''a! issobh nizilt ilbalad bi
ҫàràbiyyiti we dàwwàrt tool innàhàar.
kaan ҫandi fikra ҫan il'amaakin irrixiisà fa roht
kaza makaan. il'awwil ẓoft ẓa''iteen
sȯġàyyàriin. baҫd iddohr wi'iҫt ҫala ẓa''a
gamiila! dafaҫt il'igàar bitaaҫ awwil ẓàhr.
mafàkkàrtiẓ kitiir la'inni habbeet iẓẓa''a awi!
manimtiẓ ba'aali osbuuҫ la'inn ẓa''iti l'adiima kaanit
fi ẓaariҫ dawẓa awi!

NEW WORDS

imbaarih	yesterday
dàwwàr	to look for
tool innàhàar	all day
ҫandi fikra	I have an idea
makaan/amaakin	place
wi'iҫ	to fall
wi'iҫ ҫala	to stumble upon, to find by chance
il'igàar	the rent
la'inn	because
kaza	several (always followed by a singular noun)
awwil ẓàhr	the first month

ba'a	to stay, to remain
ba'aali	expresses duration, a length of time spent in a place.

* * * * * * * * *

TAPE XII/SIDE 2

UNIT NINE

Do this section after you have finished Unit IX.
Memorize the following dialogue, then translate it into
English. Our translation will be on the next page.
Check your work against the model answers. Now listen
and repeat:

George   —   Sally, ana laazim asaafir bokrȧ ssobh we
               maçandiiʃ ʃonȧt! açmil eeh?

Sally   —   mafiiʃ wa't çaʃaan tiʃtiri ʃonȧt
               dilwa'ti.

George   —   di moʃkila! we dȧruuri akuun fi New York
               bokrȧ!

Sally   —   yimkin iggiraan çandohom...

George   —   miʃ maç'uul! miʃ momkin naaxod ʃonȧt
               minhom.

Sally   —   kaan fiih ʃȧntiteen odaam figgȧrȧȧj,
               dȧwwȧrt kwayyis?

George   —   aywa makanʃ fiih haaga.

Sally   —   issaaça dilwa'ti hdaaʃar! mafiiʃ ġeer
               iggiraan!

George   —   ti'dȧri tis'ali inti, ya Sally?

Sally   —   leeh la'! gaayiz yidduuna waḥda. fiih
               nuur çandohom?

```
George      -    aywa, manamuuş.
Sally       -    tåyyib, çan iznak....

. . . . . . . . . . . . . . . . . . . . . . .

Sally       -    itfåddål, ya siidi!  talat şonåt!  bass
                 laazim tihaafiz çaleehom.
George      -    tåbçan.  dilwa'ti momkin aaxod koll
                 haaga! fiih makaan kifaaya fi şşonåt.
                 inti hayla ya Sally!
```

NEW WORDS

bokrå ssobh	tomorrow morning
wa't	time
iggiraan	the neighbors
miş maç'uul	impossible, incredible
ġeer	except
çan iznak	excuse me
haafiz çala	take good care of...

TRANSLATION OF THE DIALOGUE

George	-	Sally, I must leave tomorrow morning and I don't have suitcases!
Sally	-	There's no time to buy suitcases now.
George	-	This is a problem. And I must be in New York tomorrow.
Sally	-	Maybe the neighbors have some.
George	-	Impossible! We can't take suitcases from them.
Sally	-	There were two old suitcases in the garage. Did you look well?
George	-	Yes. There was nothing.
Sally	-	It is eleven o'clock now. There's no

                              one but the neighbors!

George   –   Could you ask them, Sally?

Sally   –   Why not! They might give us one. Is
               their light on?

George   –   Yes. They haven't slept.

Sally   –   OK. Excuse me.

               . . . .

Sally   –   Here you go, my dear! Three suitcases!
               But you must take good care of them.

George   –   Of course. Now I can take everything!
               There's enough space in the suitcases.
               Sally, you are outstanding.

               *   *   *   *   *   *   *   *   *

TAPE XII/SIDE 2

UNIT TEN

Do this section after you have finished Unit X.
Memorize the following passage. Start the passage
using "homma," then "ihna" and finally "ana" and make
the necessary changes each time. For the correct
answers consult units VII, VIII, IX and X of the text.
Now listen and repeat:

      çaawiz yiruuh issinima laakin maçanduuʂ wa't.
sihi waxri nnåhårdå koll yoom biynaam badri giddan,
bass imbarrih iʂtaġal kitiir billeel. laazim
yisållåh çåråbiyyitu nnåhrdå baçd iddohr çaʂaan iggårååj
hayi'fil bokrå. kamaan nifsu yilçab tenis. ya xåbår!
nisi yidfaç foluus innuur. dayman biyidfaç filmaçaad,
miʂ biyistanna li aaxir di'ii'a. yinzil dilwa'ti walla
yu'çud yiçmil ʂoġlu? haaga såçb awi! mafiiʂ
wa't çaʂaan koll ilhagaat di. yidxul yinaam ahsan!

194

NEW WORDS

sållåh/yisållåh	to repair
afal/yi'fil	to shut, to close
liçib/yilçab	to play
ya xåbår!	Oh dear!
foluus innuur	the electricity bill
dayman	always
aaxir di'ii'a	last minute
açad/yu'çud	to remain, stay sit
ahsan	better

          *   *   *   *   *   *   *   *   *

There is no self-test for Unit 11.

TAPE XII/SIDE 2

UNIT TWELVE

Do this section after you have completed the whole
textbook. This is a listening comprehension passage.
The passage, comprehension questions, and correct
answers are recorded on tape. Listen to the passage
several times before you begin answering the questions.
You will be given time on the tape to supply the answer.
You will then hear the correct answer. Please repeat
the answer you will hear on the tape. Now begin:

    çali bååbå kaan råågil fa'iir. kaan çaayiʂ liwahadu
lihadd ma aabil bint hilwa ismaha morgaana. awwil ma
ʂafha habbaha wetgawwizu çala tool! çali bååbå kaan
çandu oodå ʂoğåyyårå we howwa we morgaana çamaluuha
ganna! koll yoom çali bååbå yuxrog çaʂaan yiʂtağal we
yirgaç ilbeet billeel taçbaan, yillaa'i morgaana çamla
akl hilw awi!

mårrå kaan maaṣi biyfåkkår, simiç soot waahid
råågil biy'uul: "iftah ya simsim" çali bååbå ṣaaf baab
maġaara biyiftah liwahdu. mafiiṣ hadd fatahu! baçd
yomeen çali bååba rigiç ilmaġåårå we çamal zayy irråågil
we aal: "iftah ya simsim"!

lamma aal iggomla di, baab ilmaġåårå infatah.
daxal çali bååbå we ṣaaf hagaat ġariiba! gowwa
lmaġaara kaan fiih fluus we konuuz! çali bååbå axad
ṣwayyit hagaat we hatt fluus fi geebu! rigiç ilbeet
we idda morgaana lhidiyya di!

morgaana firhit awi we sa'alitu: "eeh da! gibt
kollda mneen?"

çali bååbå allaha: "min ilmaġåårå! la'eet kinz ya
morgaana! ilhamdu-li-llaah! dilwa'ti çandina fluus
kitiir. momkin niṣtiri beet kibiir, we niçmil illi hna
çawziin niçmilu!

NEW WORDS

fa'iir/fo'årå	poor
itgawwiz/yitgawwiz	to get married
ganna	paradise
soot/aswaat	voice
maġåårå	cave
hadd	someone
mafiiṣ hadd	there is no one
zayy	like
gomla/gomal	sentence
geeb/geyuub	pocket
kinz/konuuz	treasure

firiḥ/yifraḥ	to become happy
gaab/yigiib	to bring
mineen	where from

COMPREHENSION QUESTIONS

The questions and answers are recorded on tape. Listen
to the questions and provide the answer. You will hear
the correct answer on tape.

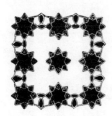

Lexicon of Useful Words and Expressions

Everyday Expressions

Arabic	English
Greetings	
såbååh ilxeer	Good morning
såbååh innuur	Good morning. (response)
masaa' ilxeer	Good evening.
masaa' innuur	Good evening. (response)
issalaamu çalaykom	Peace be upon you.
weçalaykom issalaam	May peace be upon you. (response)
saçiida	Hello!
saçiida mobååråk	Hello! (response)
izzayyak	How are you? (m.)
izzayyik	How are you? (f.)
izzayy issihhå	How is your health?
ilhamdu lillaah	Thanks be to God! (response)

Taxi Rides	
çala tuul	Go straight.
liff ʃimaal	Turn left.
liff yimiin	Turn right.
çandak	Stop right there.
oddaam ʃwayya	Up ahead.
çala nnåsyå	Round the corner.

ilçaddaad kaam?	How much is the meter?
bisorçà	Quickly.
biẓweeẓ	Slowly.

Sickness
salamtak	May you get well.
allah yissallimak	May God keep you well. (response)

Going Away
maça ssalaama	Peaceful departure!
allah yisallimak	May God keep you well.
aẓuuf wiẓẓak bixeer	May I see <u>your face</u> again well.
tirgaç bissalaama	May you return with peace.

Compliments at Meals
sallim iidik	Bless your hands.
allah yisallimik	(response)

Before and After Food
bilhana wiẓẓifa	Eat with happiness and health.
allah yihanniik	May God give you happiness.

After Drinking
haniyyan	With happiness.
allah yihanniik	

After a Meal at Someone's House

sofrå dayman	Always a plentiful table.
daamit hayaatak	May you have a long life.

Weddings, Births, Success in Exams

måbruuk	Congratualtions.
allah yibaarik fiik	God bless you.
ço'baalak	May you be given the same.

Deaths

ilba'iyya fi hayaatak	May you have a long life!
hayaatak ilba'ya	May yours be long!

Feasts

koll santa winta tåyyib	May you be well every year!
winta bissihhå wissalaama	And you be healthy and well!

Expressions of Time

English	Arabic
this year	issana di
last year	issana lli faatit
next year	issana lli gayya
this month	iššàhr da
last month	iššahr illi faat
next month	iššàhr illi gayy
today	innàhàrdà
tomorrow	bokrà
yesterday	imbaariḥ
in the morning	issobḥ
in the afternoon	baçd iddohr
in the evening	billeel
the year before last	issana lli abl illi faatit
the month before last	iššàhr illi abl illi faat
every year	koll sana
every month	koll šàhr
all day	tuul ilyoom
all year round	tuul issana
all the days	koll il'ayyaam
all the months	koll il'ošhor
all the years	koll issiniin

Names of Professions

English	Singular	Plural
doctor	doktoor (a)	dakatra
nurse	momàrridà	momàrridàåt
male nurse	tamargi	tamargiyya
mailman	bostàgi	bostàgiyya
pharmacist	agzagi	agzagiyya
dry cleaner	makwagi	makwagiyya
shoe-repairer	gazmagi	gazmagiyya
waiter	sofràgi	sofràgiyya
driver	sawwaa'	sawwa'iin
plumber	sabbaak	sabbakiin
grocer	ba''aal	ba''aliin
vender	bayyaaç	bayyaçiin
fish vender	sammaak	sammakiin
butcher	gàzzàår	gàzzàriin
pastry maker	halawaani	halawaniyya
maid	∮aġġaala	∮aġġalaat
washerwoman	ġassaala	ġassalaat
baker	fàrràån	fàrràniin
soldier	çaskari	çasaakir
officer	zàåbit	zobbàåt
army officer	zàåbit gee∮	zobbàåt gee∮
police officer	zàåbit boliis	zobbàåt boliis
doorman	bawwaab	bawwabiin

English	Singular	Plural
bellboy	fårrååʃ	fårråʃiin
middleman	simsåår	såmåsrå
engineer	mohandis (a)	mohandisiin (-aat)
carpenter	någgåår	någgåriin
barber	hallaa'	halla'iin
teacher	modarris (a)	modarrisiin (-aat)
lawyer	mohaami	mohamiyya (-aat)
judge	åådi	odååh
garbage man	zabbaal	zabbaliin
goldsmith	sååyiġ	soyyaaġ
secretary	sekerteera	sekerteraat
dressmaker	xåyyååtå	xåyyåtååt
hairdresser	kwaffer	kwaferaat
president	rå'iis	ro'åså
minister	waziir	wozårå
professor	ostaaz	asatza
assistant	mosaaçid (a)	mosaçdiin
deputy	wakiil	wokala
landlord	såhb ilbeet	åshååb ilbeyuut
pilot	tåyyår	tåyyåriin

Names of Places

English	Singular	Plural
company	ŝirka	ŝarikaat
embassy	sifaara	sifaaraat
bank	bank	bonuuk
center	markaz	maraakiz
institute	maçhad	maçaahid
university	gamça	gamçaat
district	mȧnti'a	mȧnȧti'
ministry	wizȧȧrȧ	wizȧrȧȧt
faculty	kolliyya	kolliyyaat
F. of medicine	kolliyt ittibb	
F. of engineering	kolliyt ilhandasa	
F. of fine arts	kolliyt ilfonuun iggamiila	
F. of arts	kolliyt il'adaab	
F. of political sciences	kolliyt ilçoluum issiyasiyya	
theatre	mȧsrȧh	masaarih
cinema	sinima	sinimaat
club	naadi	nawaadi
building	mabna	mabaani
apart. house	çimȧȧrȧ	çimȧrȧȧt
office	maktab	makaatib

205

English	Singular	Plural
hotel	lokåndå	lokåndååt
bar	båår	bårååt
shop	dokkan	dakakiin
store	mahall	mahallaat
restaurant	måtçåm	måtååçim
garden	gineena	ganaayin
station	måhåttå	måhåttååt
square	midaan	mayadiin
corner	nåsyå	nåwååsi
bakery	maxbaz	maxaabiz
farm	måzråçå	mazaariç
hospital	mostaşfa	mostaşfayaat
clinic	çiyaada	çiyadaat
pharmacy	agzaxaana	agzaxanaat
library	maktaba	maktabaat
kitchen	måtbåx	måtååbix
airport	måtåår	måtårååt
harbor	miina	mawaani
museum	mathaf	mataahif
temple	maçbad	maçaabid
mosque	gaamiç	gawaamiç
church	kiniisa	kanaayis
school	madrasa	madaaris

Names of Countries and Nationalities

Country	Arabic	Nationality	Plural
USA	amriika	amrikaani	amrikaan
		amrikaniyya	
France	fåránsa	fåránsaawi	fåránswiyyiin
		fåránsawiyya	(-aat)
Egypt	måsr	måsri	masriyyiin
		måsriyya	(-aat)
Japan	ilyabaan	yabaani	yabaan
		yabaniyya	
Greece	ilyonaan	yonaani	yonaan
		yonaniyya	
Germany	almania	almaani	almaan
		almaniyya	
Italy	italiya	tålyaani	tolyaan
		tålyaniyya	
Russia	rosiya	ruusi	ruus
		ruusiyya	
Lebanon	libnaan	libnaani	libnaniyyiin
		libnaniyya	
Syria	soria	suuri	suriyyiin
		suuriyya	
Israel	isra'iil	isra'iili	isra'iliyyiin
		isra'iliyya	

Palestine	filistiin	filistiini	filistiniyyiin
		filistiniyya	
England	ingiltera	ingiliizi	ingiliiz
		ingiliziyya	

Region	Arabic
the Middle East	iŝŝàrqil'awsàt
the Far East	iŝŝàrqil'àgsà
Latin America	amriika llatiiniyya
Europe	orobbà
Asia	asya
Australia	ostoràlyà

Fruits - Vegetables - Groceries

English	Arabic/(collective)	Countable
apples	toffaah	toffahaat
oranges	borto'aan	-aat
bananas	mooz	-aat
melons	battiix	-aat
mangoes	manga	-aat
figs	tiin	-aat
dates	balah	-aat
spinach	sabaanix	___
zucchini	koosa	-aat
carrots	gazar	-aat
tomatoes	tamaatim	-aat
eggplant	bitingaan	-aat
cucumber	xiyaar	-aat
peas	bisilla	-aat
onion	basal	-aat
garlic	toom	___
sugar	sukkar	
tea	saay	
coffee	bonn	
rice	rozz	
cheese	gibna	
salt	malh	
pepper	filfil	
bread	çeeş	

Public Services

English	Arabic
fire department	ilmàtàáfi
ambulance	il'isçaaf
police	ilboliis
telephone company	màslàhit ittilifonaat
power services	hay'it ikkàhràbà
sewage services	màslàhit ilmagaari
transit system	hay'it ilmowàslààt
telecommunication	ittilliġraaf

Means of Transportation

car (private)	çàràbiyyà mallaaki
car (public)	çàràbiyyà ogrà
tramway	torommàày
train	àtr (otora)
bicycle	çagala (çagal)
airplane	tàyyààrà (-aat)
ship	markib (maraakib)
bus	otobiis (-aat)
means of transportation	mowààsàlààt

Glossary

English/Arabic

ENGLISH	ARABIC
A	
to accompany	wàssàl
actually	filha'ii'a
address	çinwaan çanawiin (pl.)
to admire	çagab (v.)
after	baçd (baçd ma)
afternoon	baçd iddohr
afterwards	baçdeen
again	taani /màrrà tania
to agree	waafi' (v.)
agriculture	ziraaça
airplane	tàyyàrà tàyyàràat (pl.)
airport	màtàar màtàràat (pl.)
all	koll
almost	ta'riiban, hawaali
alone	liwahd- i / u/ aha...etc.
also	kamaan
always	dayman
and	we
another	taani (another day = yoom taani)
to answer	gaawib, ràdd (cala)
answer	ràdd, igaaba /roduud (pl.),

	igabaat (pl.)
apartment	ƃa''a ƃo'a' (pl.)
to appear	záhár
appearance	mázhár mázááhir (pl.)
appointment	maçaad mawaçiid (pl.)
approximately	ta'riiban, hawaali
Arabs	çáráb
Arabic	çárábi
area	mánti'á mánááti' (pl.)
arm	diraaç diraçaat (pl.)
around	hawaleen
arrive	wásál
art	fann fonuun (pl.)
artisan	sánáyçi sánáyçiyya (pl.)
as	zayy
as soon as	awwil ma
ashtray	tá'tuu'á, táffááyá
to ask	sa'al
to ask for	sa'al çala
at	çand
aunt (maternal)	xaala
aunt (paternal)	çamma

B

back	dáhr
bag	ƃántá ƃonát (pl.)
banana	mooza mooz (pl.)
bank	bank bonuuk (pl.)
basket	sabat sibita (pl.)

to be	kaan (v.)
beans	fuul
to beat	dàràb (v.)
because	caşaan, la'inn
bed	seriir saraayir (pl.)
bedroom	ooditnoom owàdnoom (pl.)
before	abl /abl ma
behind	wàrà
beside	gamb
better	ahsan
big	kibiir kobààr (pl.)
birthday	çiid milaad
blouse	bluuza bluzaat (pl.)
book	kitaab kotob (pl.)
boss	modiir modiriin (pl.)
bottle	izaaza azaayiz (pl.)
to bother	dayyi' (v.)
boy	walad awlaad (pl.)
brain	moxx amxaax (pl.)
bread	çeeş
to break	kàsàr (v.)
to breakfast	fitir (v.)
breakfast	fitààr
bride	çàruusà çàrààyis (pl.)
bridegroom	çariis çirsaan (pl.)
to bring	gaab (v.)
broker	simsààr sàmàsrà (pl.)
brother	àxx oxwaat (pl.)
to build	bana (v.)

213

building	mabna	mabaani (pl.)
butler	sofrảgi	sofrảgiyya (pl.)
butter	zibda	
to buy	iŝtara	(v.)

C

calm	haadi	hadyiin (pl.)
car	çảrảbiyyả	çảrảbiyyảảt (pl.)
to carry	ŝaal	(v.)
case	ảḍiyyả	ảḍảảyả (pl.)
cat	ottả	otảṭ (pl.)
cave	mảġảảrả	mảġảrảảt (pl.)
to catch	misik	(v.)
city	madiina	modon (pl.)
chair	korsi	karaasi (pl.)
chance	forsả	forảs (pl.)
change	taġyiir	taġyiraat (pl.)
to change	ġảyyảr	(v.)
cheap	rixiis	roxảảs (pl.)
cheese	gibna	giban (pl.)
cheque	ŝeek	ŝekaat (pl.)
church	kiniisa	kanaayis (pl.)
cigarette	sigảảrả	sagaayir (pl.)
cinema	sinima	sinimaat (pl.)
clean	nidiif	nodảảf (pl.)
to clean	nảddảf	(v.)
clever	ŝảảtr	ŝảtriin (pl.)
clock	saaça	saçaat (pl.)
to close	afal	(v.)
close	orảyyib min, gamb	

clothes	hoduum
club	naadi nawaadi (pl.)
cockroach	sorsȧȧr sȧrȧsiir (pl.)
coffee	ahwa
coffee shop	ahwa ahaawi (pl.)
comb	miẓt ȧmẓȧȧt (pl.)
cold	bard
to come	geh (v.)
color	loon alwaan (pl.)
comfortable	moriih
company	ẓirka ẓarikaat (pl.)
congratulations	mȧbruuk
contract	ça'd ço'uud (pl.)
to cook	tȧbȧx (v.)
cook	tȧbbȧȧx tȧbbȧxiin (pl.)
cost	taman
to count	çadd (v.)
country	balad bilaad (pl.)
to cover	ġȧttȧ (v.)
cover	ġȧtȧ ġotyȧȧn (pl.)
to crave	nifsi fi
crowded	zahma
cucumbers	xiyȧȧr
customer	zobuun zabaayin (pl.)
to cut	ȧtȧç (v.)
cute	hilw, zȧriif hilwiin, zorȧȧf (pl.)

D

dark	dȧlmȧ	
day	yoom	ayyaam (pl.)
dear	çaziiz	çozaaz (pl.)
debt	deen	deyuun (pl.)
death	moot	
desert	sȧhȧrȧ	sȧhri (pl.)
desk	maktab	makaatib (pl.)
difficult	sȧçb	
to dine	itçaṣṣa (v.)	
dinner	çaṣa	
distance	masaafa	masafaat (pl.)
district	hayy	ahaa' (pl.)
drawer	dorg	ȧdrȧȧg (pl.)
to dress	libis (v.)	
dress	fostaan	fasatiin (pl.)
dressmaker	xȧyyȧȧtȧ	xȧyyȧtȧȧt (pl.)
to drink	ṣirib (v.)	
doctor	doktoor	dakatra (pl.)
to do	çamal (v.)	
dog	kalb	kilaab (pl.)
door	baab	abwaab (pl.)
doorman	bawwaab	bawwabiin (pl.)
downstairs	taht	
downtown	wist ilbalad	
dumb	ġabi	aġbiya (pl.)

E

ear	widn	widaan (pl.)
early	badri	

216

easy	sahl
to eat	kal, akal (v.)
economics	iqtisáàd
egg	beedà beed (pl.)
Egypt	màsr
elbow	kuuç kiçaan (pl.)
electricity	kàhràbà
emergency	tàwààri'
employee	mowàzzàf mowàzzàfiin (pl.)
empty	fààdi fàdyiin (pl.)
engine	motoor mawatiir (pl.)
engineer	mohanddis mohandisiin (pl.)
enough	kifaaya
to enter	daxal (v.)
entrance	madxal madaaxil (pl.)
to entertain	salla (v.)
envelope	zàrf ozrof, zoruuf (pl.)
Eve	hawwa
evening	billeel
every	koll
exactly	bizzàbt
excellent	momtaaz momtaziin (pl.)
except	illa, çeer, ma çada
exercise	tamriin tamrinaat (pl.)
to exit	xàràg (v.)
expensive	ġaali ġalyiin (pl.)
explain	ʃàràh (v.)
explanation	ʃàrh
export	sàddàr (v.)
eye	çeen çeneen (pl.)

F

face	wiśś	wośuuś (pl.)
factory	màsnàç	màsàániç
to fall	wi'iç (v.)	
family	çeela	çelaat (pl.)
far	beçiid	
far from	beçiid çan	
farm	çezba	çezab (pl.)
father	àbb	àbbàhààt (pl.)
to fear	xaaf (v.)	
fence	suur	àswààr (pl.)
to find	la'a (v.)	
figs	tiin	
to finish	xàllàs (v.)	
fish	samak	
floor	àrd	
flour	di'ii'	
fly	dibbaana	dibbaan (pl.)
to fly	tààr (v.)	
food	akl	
for	çaśaan, li	
to forbid	manaç (v.)	
forbidden	mamnuuç	
foreigner	agnabi	agaanib (pl.)
to forget	nisi (v.)	
fork	śooka	śowak (pl.)
friend	sààhib	àshààb (pl.)
from	min	
fruit	fakha	
to fry	ala (v.)	

218

full	malyaan	malyaniin (pl.)
full stomach	ṣabҫaan	ṣabҫaniin (pl.)
funeral	ganaaza	ganazaat (pl.)
funny	modhik	modhikiin (pl.)
furthermore	ҫilaawa ҫala kida	

G

garden	geneena	ganaayin (pl.)
gardener	ganayni	ganayniyya (pl.)
garage	gàràaj	gàràjàat (pl.)
gas	banziin	
to gather	lamm (v.)	
general	liwa	liwa'aat (pl.)
in general	ҫomuuman, ҫaamatan	
girl	bint	banaat (pl.)
to give	idda (v.)	
glass	izaaz	
a glass	kobbaaya	kobbayaat (pl.)
to go	miṣi, ràah (v.)	
to go down	nizil (v.)	
to go home	ràwwàh (v.)	
to go out	xàràg (v.)	
to go up	tiliҫ (v.)	
god	àllààh, ilaah	
good	kwayyis	kwayyisiin (pl.)
to govern	hakam (v.)	
government	hokuuma	hokumaat (pl.)
grandfather	gidd	agdaad (pl.)
grandmother	gidda	giddaat (pl.)

grocer	ba''aal ba''aliin (pl.)
groceries	bi'aala
guest	deef deyuuf (pl.)
guilty	moznib moznibiin (pl.)

H

half	noss
happy	saçiid soçada (pl.)
hat	borneeta barániit (pl.)
to have	çand
he	howwa
to hear	simiç (v.)
heavy	ti'iil to'aal (pl.)
hell	gohannam, innáár
here	hina
here (is)	aho..ahe..ahom
high	caali çalyiin (pl.)
honey	çasal
hot	(weather) hárr; (things) soxn
hotel	lokándá, fondoq lokándáát, fanaadi' (pl.)
hour	saaça sacaat (pl.)
house	beet beyuut (pl.)
how	izzaay
How are you?	izzayyak?
however	çala ayy haal
how much	add eeh
how many	kaam
human	insaani
human being	insaan, šáxs, bani aadam

hungry	gaçaan gaçaniin (pl.)
husband	gooz agwaaz (pl.)

I

I	ana
idea	fikra afkåår (pl.)
if	iza, law, in
immediately	haalan, çala tool
to import	istawrid (v.)
import	istiirååd
importance	ahammiyya
important	mohimim mohimmiin (pl.)
incredible	mi$ maç'uul
injury	garh goruuh (pl.)
innocent	barii' abriyaa' (pl.)
inside	gowwa
to insult	$atam, ahaan (v.)
insult	$itiima, ihaana
international	dawli
to invite	çazam çala (v.)
invitation	çozuuma çazaayim (pl.)
to iron	kawa (v.)
iron	makwa makaawi (pl.)
iron (metal)	hådiid

J

jail	sign soguun (pl.)
jam	maråbbå
jasmine	yasmiin
joke	nokta nokat (pl.)

judge	ȧȧdi	odȧȧh (pl.)
juice	çȧsiir	
just	lissa	

K

to keep	xalla (v.)	
key	moftaah	mafatiih (pl.)
kilo	kiilo	
king	malik	moluuk (pl.)
kingdom	mamlaka	mamaalik (pl.)
knee	rokba	rokab (pl.)
knife	sikkiina	sakakiin (pl.)
to know	çirif (v.)	
knowledge	çilm, miçrifa	

L

land	ȧrd	ȧrȧȧdi (pl.)
language	loġa	loġaat (pl.)
late	waxri, mit'ȧxxȧr	
law	qȧnuun	qȧwaniin (pl.)
lawyer	mohaami	mohamiyiin (pl.)
lazy	kaslaan	kaslaniin (pl.)
to leave	miǥi, saafir (v.)	
left	ǥimaal	
leg	rigl	rigleen (pl.)
lesson	dars	doruus (pl.)
library	maktaba	makaatib (pl.)
to light	wallaç (v.)	
light	nuur	ȧnwȧȧr (pl.)
light (adj.)	xafiif	xofaaf (pl.)

lighter	wallaaça	wallaçaat (pl.)
to like	ḥabb (v.)	
like	zayy, zayyma	
to listen	simiç (v.)	
to live	çaaʃ (v.)	
living room	oodit maçiiʃa	
to look	bảss (v.)	
to look at	bảss li	
to look for	dảwwảr çala (v.)	
lonely	waḥiid	
to lose	dảyyảç (v.)	
to love	ḥabb (v.)	
to lunch	itġadda (v.)	
lunch	ġada	

M

maid	ʃaġġaala	ʃaġġalaat (pl.)
to make	çamal (v.)	
man	rảảgil	riggaala (pl.)
to manage	itsảrrảf (v.)	
manager	modiir	modiriin (pl.)
many	kitiir	
market	suu'	aswaa' (pl.)
married	mitgawwiz	mitgawwiziin (pl.)
marriage	gawaaz	
to marry	itgawwiz (v.)	
may	momkin	
meat	laḥma	
to meet	aabil (v.)	

meeting	igtimaaç	igtimaçaat (pl.)
meter	mitr	ȧmtȧȧr (pl.)
middleman	simsȧȧr	sȧmȧsrȧ (pl.)
midwife	daaya	dayaat (pl.)
might	yimkin, gaayiz, iḥtimaal	
milk	laban	
mind	moxx	amxaax (pl.)
minister	waziir	wozȧrȧ (pl.)
minute	di'ii'a	da'aayi' (pl.)
money	foluus	
month	šȧhr	ošhor (pl.)
mosque	gaaamiç	gawaamiç (pl.)
most	moçzȧm	
mother	omm	ommahaat (pl.)
mouse	fȧȧr	firaan (pl.)
movie	film	aflaam (pl.)
mud	ṭiin	
must	laazim, ḍȧruuri	

N

name	ism	asaami (pl.)
narrow	dayya'	dayya'iin (pl.)
near	orȧyyib, gamb	
nearby	orȧyyib min	
neighbors	giraan (pl.)	
neither ... nor	la ... wala	
nerves	ȧçsȧȧb	
nervous	çȧsȧbi	
new	gidiid	godaad (pl.)

nevertheless	çala ayy haal
nice	zåriif zoråaf (pl.)
noisy	dawṣa
noise	dawṣa
noon	iddohr
no one	wala hadd
nose	manaxiir
nothing	wala haaga
noun	ism
now	dilwa'ti
nowadays	ilyomeen dool
number	nimra nimar (pl.)

O

office	maktab makaatib (pl.)
officer	zåabit zobbåat (pl.)
oil	zeet
old	(things) adiim odaam (pl.)
	(people) çaguuz çawagiiz (pl.)
on	çala
one	waahid (m.) wahda (f.)
once	mårrå
only	bass, wahiid
to open	fatah (v.)
or	aw
to order	tålåb (v.)
to order someone to do ...	åmår (v.)
outside	bårrå

outstanding	haayil, ċaziim	
oven	forn	àfràȧn (pl.)

P

page	sàfhȧ	sàfhȧȧt (pl.)
pan	tȧȧsȧ	tȧsȧȧt (pl.)
paper	wara'a	wara' (pl.)
paradise	igganna	
partner	¢iriik	¢orȧkȧ (pl.)
to pass	faat (v.)	
to pass by	faat ċala ... (v.)	
to pass exam	niċih (v.)	
to pay	dafaċ (v.)	
peasant	fallaah	fallahiin (pl.)
pen	alam hibr	
pencil	alam rosȧȧs	ilima (pl.)
people	naas	
pepper	filfil	
picture	suurȧ	sowȧr (pl.)
plate	tȧbȧ'	tobȧȧ' (pl.)
to play	liċib (v.)	
player	laaċib	laċiibi (pl.)
please	min fȧdlȧk	
pocket	geeb	geyuub (pl.)
politics	siyaasa	
poor	fa'iir	fo'ȧrȧ (pl.)
porter	¢ayyaal	¢ayyaliin (pl.)
possible	momkin	
prayer	sȧlȧȧ	sȧlȧwaat (pl.)
priest	assiiss	osos (pl.)

present	mawguud	mawgudiin (pl.)
president	rå'iis	ro'åså (pl.)
pretty	hilw	hilwiin (pl.)
problem	moṣkila	maṣaakil (pl.)
professor	ostaaz	asatza (pl.)
to push	za'' (v.)	
to put	hått (v.)	
pyramid	håråm	åhrååm (pl.)

Q

quarter	robç	irbaç (pl.)
quarter (place)	hayy	ahyaa' (pl.)
queen	malika	malikaat (pl.)
question	su'aal	as'ila (pl.)
quickly	bisorçå	

R

radio	rådyo
rain	måtårå
to rain	måttår (v.)
to read	årå (v.)
reason	sabab asbaab (pl.)
reasonable	maç'uul
refrigerator	tallaaga tallagaat (pl.)
to remember	iftåkår (v.)
to remind	fåkkår (v.)
to rent	åggår (v.)
rent	iigåår igårååt (pl.)
to repair	sållåh (v.)
to repent	taab (v.)

repentance	tooba
to reside	sikin (v.)
responsible	mas'uul mas'uliin (pl.)
responsibility	mas'uliyya
rest (the)	ilbaa'i
to rest	istirayyah (v.)
restaurant	måtçåm måtååçim (pl.)
reward	mokaf'a mokaf'aat (pl.)
to reward	kaafi' (v.)
rice	rozz
rich	ġani aġniya (pl.)
to ride	rikib (v.)
right	yimiin
right (correct)	såhh
to rise	aam, tiliç (the sun rose = iṡṡams tilçit)
room	oodå owåd (pl.)
rose water	maward

S

sale	okazyoon okazyonaat (pl.)
salt	malh
to say	aal (v.)
school	madrasa madaaris (pl.)
second	sanya sawaani (pl.)
secretary	sekerteera sekerteraat (pl.)
to see	ṡaaf (v.)
to sell	baaç (v.)
sentence	gomla gomal (pl.)

servant	xaddaam xaddamiin (pl.)
several	kaza
to sew	xȧyyȧt (v.)
shirt	ȧmiis omsȧȧn (pl.)
she	hiyya
shoe	gazma gizam (pl.)
shop	mahall, dokkaan mahallaat, dakakiin (pl.)
short	osȧyyȧr osȧyyȧriin (pl.)
should	laazim
to show	warra, fȧrrȧg (v.)
shower	doʃʃ
to shower	istahamma (v.)
single	çaazib çozzaab (pl.)
sister	oxt oxwaat (pl.)
to sit	açad (v.)
to sleep	naam (v.)
sleep	noom
slow	bȧtii' botȧ'ȧ (pl.)
slowly	biʃweeʃ
small	soġȧyyȧr soġȧyyȧriin (pl.)
smell	riiha
to smell	ʃamm
smile	ibtisaama ibtisamaat (pl.)
to smile	ibtasam (v.)
social	igtimaaci
so	fa
sofa	kanaba kanab (pl.)
some	ʃwayya

something	haaga
to speak	itkallim (v.)
speech (a)	xotbå xotåb (pl.)
to spend	såråf (v.)
spoon	maçla'a maçaali' (pl.)
station	måhåttå måhåttååt (pl.)
to steal	sara' (v.)
steel	solb
still	lissa
story	hikaaya hikayaat (pl.)
stomach	båtn botuun (pl.)
strange	ġariib ġurååb (pl.)
street	ŝaariç ŝawaariç (pl.)
to stop	wi'if (v.)
to study	zaakir (v.)
sugar	sokkår
suit	badla bidal (pl.)
summer	seef

T

table	tåråbeezå tåråbezååt (pl.)
to take	xad, axad (v.)
tailor	tarzi tarziyya (pl.)
tall	tåwiil towåål (pl.)
to teach	darris (v.)
teacher	modarris modarrisiin (pl.)
telegram	telleġraaf telleġrafaat (pl.)
telephone	tilifoon tilifonaat (pl.)
telephone call	mokalma mokalmaat (pl.)
television	tilivizyoon tilivizyonaat (pl)

to tell	haka (v.)
to test	imtahan (v.)
test	imtihaan imtihanaat (pl.)
than	min
thanks	motaşakkir, şokrán
that	da, di, dool
that	inn-i /ak/ik ... etc.
theater	másráh masaarih (pl.)
thief	háráámi hárámiyyá (pl.)
there	hinaak
there is/are	fiih
these	dool
they	homma
thing	haaga hagaat (pl.)
to think	fákkár fi (v.)
this	da
third	tilt
thread	xeet xeyuut (pl.)
time	wa't aw'aat (pl.)
tired	taçbaan taçbaniin (pl.)
to	li
too	kamaan
today	innáhárdá
tomorrow	bokrá
to travel	saafir (v.)
trip	rihla
treasure	kinz konuuz (pl.)
to try	haawil (v.)

towel	footå fowåt (pl.)
typewriter	aala katba

U

uncle (maternal)	xaal xilaan (pl.)
uncle (paternal)	çamm çimaam (pl.)
under	taht
to understand	fihim (v.)
to undress	alaç (v.)
unfurnished	fådyå, miş mafruuşa
university	gamça gamçaat (pl.)
until	liġaayit ma, lihadd ma
upset	zaclaan, ġådbåån zaçlaniin, ġådbåniin (pl.)
upstairs	foo'

V

vacuum cleaner	maknasa makaanis (pl.)
vegetables	xodåår
very	awi, giddan, xåålis
village	qårya qorå (pl.)
visit	ziyåårå ziyårååt (pl.)
voice	soot aswååt (pl.)

W

wait	istanna (v.)
waiter	gårsoon gårsonååt (pl.)
to wake up	sihi (v.)
to want	çaaz (v.)
water	måyyå

watch	saaça saçaat (pl.)
to watch	itfárrág çala (v.)
we	iḥna
what	eeh
when?	imta
when	lamma
where?	feen
where	mátràḥ ma, makaan ma
which?	anhi
which	illi
while	lamma
white	ábyàd (m.) beedà (f.)
	biiḍ (pl.)
who?	miin
who	illi
whose?	bitaaç miin
why	leeh
wide	waasiç wasçiin (pl.)
wife of	mirààt, hàràm ...
wind	hawa
window	šibbaak šababiik (pl.)
with	maça, wayya
woman	sitt sittaat (pl.)
work	šoġl
to work	ištaġal (v.)
worker	çaamil çommaal (pl.)
word	kilma kalimaat (pl.)
wound	garḥ goruuh (pl.)

Y

year	sana	siniin (pl.)
yes	aywa	
yesterday	imbaariḥ	
yet	lissa	
you	inta	
you (pl.)	intu